# SHUT YOUR MOUTH WHEN YOU'RE TALKING TO ME

*For my momma*

"Help others, protect children, love animals, speak the truth, say please and thank you, say fuck you when necessary, dress-up, use the good silverware, light the expensive candle, eat the whole can of pringles, take a nap in the sunshine, adopt a foster child, don't diet, do diet, be daring, volunteer, say your prayers, read more, be honest, be forthcoming, say what you mean, protect others feelings, live boldly, don't be racist, respect other religions, swear a lot if you want to, decorate everything, smoke cigarettes, laugh and laugh and laugh, don't let your past define your future, don't be a shitty friend, be optimistic and believe that everything is possible, respect yourself, trust yourself, make lots of photo albums, be original, stop and smell the roses, live every day like it's your last, hug your husband like you mean it and kiss your children right on the lips!"

-Ellie O'Connell

*Shut Your Mouth When You're Talking To M*e is a work of nonfiction. Some names have been changed. Some events have been condensed. But nothing was made up.

# CONTENTS

Getting a tattoo at 16... and so it is.

# Introduction

When I was a kid, my mom used to wake up an hour or so before me. She would sit on the floor in front of the heater and drink her coffee. Lots of cream, lots of sugar. The same way I take mine now. She would call a friend or my grandma and somehow talk for an entire hour about what had happened in the twelve hours since they previously spoke. She would be wearing her cashmere robe that had a few red wine stains on it but smelled like Narciso Rodriguez for Her. On weekends, we would eat crispy bacon while she responded to emails and I watched Lizzie Mcguire.

I thought life was going to go on like this forever. I could picture it so clearly.

Then, I lost her when I was 21 years old. It still doesn't feel real. I sometimes even forget that she died. I sometimes think, "Oh, her being dead is just temporary," before I'm reminded that it is in fact, permanent. Unless you're a Scientologist. I don't know how to deal with grief. I haven't even dealt with my own yet. The only advice I can give you if you've lost someone you love, is go to Cheesecake Factory whenever you want. It will help.

I hope you find what you're looking for in this book. If you're looking for a how-to guide on dealing with the loss of a loved one, this book is not for you. If you're here to figure out which Parisian cafe has the best cafe au lait, it's Starbucks. If you're here for stories about me and my mom getting into trouble, welcome.

Writing this book made me look back at events in my life and think, maybe I should have done that differently. But, if I always did the right thing, it wouldn't make for a very interesting read. I took my mom for granted. Or as I used to say, for granite. I was mean to her, really mean. But I also told her I loved her 8 to 1,500 times a day. She was also mean to me though, she took a photo of me sleeping once!

Am I being dramatic for writing a whole book about myself? I don't have a rags to riches story nor can I impart my wisdom of the New York Stock Exchange (Buy low, sell high!) nor have I ever escaped a kidnapping. I believe I have avoided getting kidnapped many times though, so if you want that story, call me. I basically wrote a book about my mom. Everyone has a mom, and no one writes a whole book about theirs. But my mom was the best mom. No offense, but you also probably wouldn't be reading this book if you didn't agree with me.

I always get compared to my mom, "You are so your mother!". I would roll my eyes and ask, "Ya, but skinnier right?" I was so embarrassed to be my mother's daughter. She wasn't like the other moms. Why couldn't I have a normal mom who stayed at home all day and made me Duncan Hines brownies? Why did my mom insist on taking me to Paris instead of my class trip to Washington D.C? Why didn't we have one BarcaLounger in our whole goddamn house? But ya know what, even though I didn't get a whole lot of time with her, we had the best time.

I'm 24 now and eating a Lunchable while I write. Those little yellow pre-packed lunches, that you were never allowed to have as a kid. I bought the pizza one, it's just three pieces of bread, tomato sauce, and shredded cheddar cheese. It's delicious. It even has a mini Crunch bar for dessert.

My mom always packed my lunches for school. It was usually a pb&j, orange slices, and a Capri Sun. Other kids had Doritos and chicken tenders, things I wasn't allowed to have unless my mom was craving them too.

One day I asked her to pack me a "fun" lunch. I was tired of never having anything to trade with. I opened my brown paper bag in front of the entire lunch table, nervous but excited to see what I would be gifted with today. I pulled out a can of tuna, package of relish and a hard-boiled egg. There was a note inside too, "your favorites!"

I quickly tried to shove the contents back into where they came from, but it was too late, everyone saw. *How dare she,* I thought as the tuna can rolled back out of the bag. These were my *private* favorite foods. The kinds you eat hiding under the covers, not at your first week of second grade.

"I hate you!" I screamed as I got into the backseat of the car.

"You don't hate me, I'm your mom," She replied as she pulled out of the pickup zone.

"I hate you *because* you're my mom!"

Your mother is the only person you're allowed to hate. You can hate her for making you a social suicide lunch. You can hate her for the way she makes you wear jeans that cover your butt crack. You can hate her for the way she says Pinterest. But at the end of the day, you're going to want her to scratch your back and tell you a story about a ladybug until you fall asleep. Love your mom because she's the only person who will love you no matter what. And one day, she won't be there to embarrass you anymore, and I promise you, you will miss her.

# Don't Make Me Cry In Public

"Is Prague a country or a city?" I asked the moment I walked through the front door. My mom and I had just moved to a new apartment in Manhattan, and while beautiful, it wasn't exactly spacious. In fact, it was technically a one-bedroom that my mom had divided into two with a makeshift wall. I drew the short end of the stick and the side of the room with no windows. I had contacted CPS when I found this out and was told to "stick it out." This city had no compassion.

"What do you mean?" my mom asked, looking up from the magazine she was reading on the couch.

"What do you mean, what do I mean? Is Prague a country or a city?" I demanded.

"It's in Europe."

"Yeah, but what is it?"

"Why do you need to know? You're not going there."

"I might! We were learning about it in class today and I couldn't admit that I didn't know what Prague was," I said. "Especially because I made a comment that implied I had been there before."

"What?" my mom asked, walking the few feet to the kitchen to make some snacks. My after-school snacks were part of our contract. I needed sustenance from my long day of braiding my hair during class.

"I said that there's a great falafel place in Prague where the falafel is the size of your head," I said. "I told them I had a photo of it. Have you seen it?" I asked my mom, unaware that I was lying.

"There is no picture! You've never been to Prague!"

"I don't know if I have or not! Depends on if it's a city or a place!"

Our discussion made a sharp left and got stupider and stupider until I finally googled "Prague." It's a city. I wasn't expecting that. I yelled the answer from my bedroom to the living room to inform my mom of this revelation.

"I know!" She shouted back. No, she didn't.

After I learned that Prague was in the Czech Republic and not known for falafel, like I had convinced my classmates at my all-girls Catholic School, I started to get hungry. Reading about food makes me hungry just like watching someone get into bed in a movie makes me tired. I'm a walking talking marketers dream. I'll buy anything as long as it is on tv. Whether it's a Scientology membership or a Shake Weight, I want it.

I exited my room and made my way to the kitchen to collect my snack that I assumed would be carrots and sliced cucumbers, an anorexics dream. I was pudgy and did not appreciate the lack of chips and cookies in our household. That said, the surplus of healthy fruits and vegetables in our fridge was probably the result of me saying that I couldn't see my feet when I showered. To my surprise, my snack was not ready. My mom was struggling to open the container of hummus. She kept putting her hand into position, but nothing happened. The lid would not budge.

"Let me do it," I said, easily opening the lid. Then I stuck my index finger in to scoop off the oily layer on top, the best part.

Only recently, I'd noticed that something was wrong with my

mom. She hadn't vocalized any of her struggles to me, but there was something different. She couldn't complete little tasks that she started around the house. The framed photos that she had planned to hang, sat on the floor. I also noticed her walk was different. Once a great speed walker and crowd weaver, she was slower and walked alongside the old men rather than pushing through them. Sometimes they even lapped her.

We had discussed her symptoms very briefly and come to the conclusion that she had MS. We laughed about this, saying she would probably poop her pants. But it was all still a joke up to us at this point. I also diagnosed her with stage 6 chlamydia, that was probably the reason her walk was wonky.

After a few months of unexplainable symptoms, she began to visit multiple doctors around the city. My grandma and my mom's sister, Heather accompanied her to these appointments. For some reason, it didn't seem to strike me as unusual that they were always in town visiting. My grandma lived in Palm Springs and Heather lived in Charleston, neither of which is a quick flight away from New York. I just thought they were super into hanging out with me, probably because I was too stupid to realize something was wrong. I only went to one doctor's appointment with my mom during that time. Dr. S was an acupuncturist working out of his spare bedroom on the Lower East Side. My mom had been to this same appointment a week earlier so she knew the drill: strip down to your underwear and lay face down on the massage table. I have always been afraid of needles and couldn't wrap my head around the fact that my mom was choosing to have hundreds of them placed into her back, ass cheeks and head. Yes, her head! What I didn't know was that she was desperate. Desperate for any treatment that might give her a fighting chance, and if needles were the solution, so be it.

The acupuncturist instructed her to relax for the next 30 minutes without moving. Then, he left, closing the door behind him, expecting her to relax even though she looked like the movie poster for Hellraiser.

I got up from the chair I'd been sitting across the room and got down on the floor underneath the massage table. I laid on my back staring up at my mom's face, which was smashed in the toilet seat shaped hole in the headrest.

"What is this supposed to do?" I asked.

"It's going to make me walk better." She said barely able to move her lips in the headrest.

"Does it hurt?"

"No, I can't feel it really. You should try it. It might help your posture."

"No thank you." I politely declined. She was always on my case about my bad posture and I wanted none of it. I was not at the age where I was proud enough of my boobs to even think about standing up straight.

"Why don't we go to the Natural History Museum after this?" she suggested.

"Do we have to?"

"Yes."

I wiggled out from under the table and inspected what looked like a heat lamp.

"What does this do?" I asked.

"I don't know, don't touch it," she said, unable to see what I was doing because she couldn't move.

One of my daily complaints is that I'm cold and the other is that I'm too hot. I obviously was going to touch it and perhaps use it to heat up my hair. I loved it when my hair was warm but didn't have the strength to constantly blow dry it. I plugged in the heat lamp and sat under it with a smile.

The doctor came back in after what smelled like his smoke break and began to pull the needles out of my mom's back. He shot me a look to stop touching his things or else he'd give put me on the table next. Her back twitched every time a needle was removed but she kept saying that she was ok. She was then instructed to redress and come back next week.

"I'll see what I can move around," I informed the doctor.

"You don't need to come," he said, showing us the door.

On our way to the Natural History Museum, my mom was practically skipping. The next few days were good for her. She no longer had a limp or any difficulty in her legs and her hands were even stronger than before. I swear she turned green like the Incredible Hulk too. She began to believe that all her newfound issues could be cured by this magical acupuncturist. All talk of MS or any illness at all went out the window. She began to visit him religiously.

Until, one day she didn't. I wasn't aware that she had learned the true issue that was wreaking havoc on her body, that I was foolishly going about life thinking all was good in my hood.

I got home from school one afternoon and my mom walked into my hole of a room and asked if I wanted to go on a walk in Central Park. I knew that this walk would allow me the opportunity to pass not one but two separate hot dog stands, so my chances of getting one were higher than usual. One of my favorite things about New York is the endless supply of hotdogs.

A walk together used to be a normal after school activity when I was in elementary school, but maybe that was because we lived in beautiful Santa Barbara, California, where people liked each other. This New York thing was making us cold and distant. Physically too, this was the first time I ever had to wear a coat on a regular basis. One of the ways my mom got me to be happy about the big move, was the promise of a new peacoat from J Crew, the adult section. At just five feet tall, I was small enough to still fit into Baby Gap throughout high school. I was legally an elf but not small enough to be cast in any Christmas movies. This excited my mom but caused me to spend countless hours cutting out the tags on my kids' brand clothing and sewing on new ones. I wore a lot of Ann Taylor loft for a 14 year old.

"Extra mustard and extra relish," I said in a quiet voice to the man taking my hotdog out of lukewarm bathwater. I didn't want all the girls at school to overhear, in case one was walking by. Once my hotdog craving was curbed, we started our walk into Central Park. We went farther than we normally do and found a bench and sat down. It was warm. I had my cute summer school uniform on so I was feeling good. During the winter we wore these ankle-length plaid skirts, really outdoing the typical sister wife look. But, in the summer, we got to wear these short blue cotton skirts and white polo shirts. I was the only girl who would wear a monogrammed Ralph Lauren polo, because of my fear of making it on the worst dressed list.

"Do you think this skirt would look cute with a t-shirt like on weekends?" I asked looking at my uniform skirt. "A white t-shirt and then sneakers?" I pressed on.

My mom ignored my question and put her hand on my leg and looked right at me. She was trying to comfort me about something, I just didn't know what yet. She had a habit of turning regular conversations into serious moments. Just weeks earlier, she took me to this same bench to tell me that I needed to walk my dog Leo more now that she was a working woman.

"Gracie, we need to talk," she said, breaking the eye contact. Nothing was scarier than this phrase. I braced myself as I waited for her to ask for a divorce.

I had no idea that this was my last moment of pure innocence. I wish I would have cherished it, but that's the issue with a linear timeline. You don't know how good you have it, until it's all over.

"So you know that backache I've had lately?" My mom treaded

carefully, making a lump well up in my throat immediately. Any talk of illness makes me cry, or any talk of anything almost, can make me cry.

"Yeah, why?" I said, trying not to make eye contact.

"Well, I think I may have a nerve problem."

I already started to cry, something just felt wrong, even though barely ten words had been spoken, "What, what do you mean. What do you have?" I said wiping the tears and leftover mustard from my face. Why did she have to do this in public? I had worked very hard on not crying in public and now my streak was over. I had cried at Disneyland a few years ago and was not going to be known as "that girl" anymore.

"No no no it's ok, I'm fine. It's just a small nerve problem, but I'm going to be ok. I'm going to get it fixed. There's a doctor in Paris that can fix it," she said backtracking.

"Why does everything have to involve France in our life!" I shouted through tears. But those were the words I hung onto, my clues. I knew there was more to this than she was leading on.

We walked back to the apartment, differently than we had before. Well, she still had the limp but I kinda had it too. I walked next to her, not in front of her as I had before. I knew something was wrong and it was my job, actually my right, to find out what she was talking about via the internet. We carried on that night as if nothing were wrong, we even ordered our favorite take out from Pastrami Queen. A pastrami sandwich is scientifically proven to cure any form of discomfort.

But that night, as everyone was asleep, I simply Googled, French nerve disease and I found something called ALS. Never heard of it before, I thought it was ASL, age, sex, location, but wait we weren't on Omegle. I dug deeper into this ALS k-hole I saw that people who get it have 2 to 5 years to live.

*Wow I'm so happy this isn't what my mom has,* I thought. After all, she had to have something else because she said she was going to be okay. And we were never that 1% of people that get something. Then I thought about my mom really having ALS, putting on this show for myself crying and being all dramatic alone in the dark. I was trying to imagine the worst-case scenario, so whatever the truth was, it wouldn't be as bad as what I was pretending she had.

The next morning things felt normal again and my mom and I continued on with life. Or so I thought. I began to notice my mom struggling even more than before. Not only did I have to help with opening jars, but basic things like stirring pasta and holding boxes, things that she used to do for me on an everyday basis.

My mom had recently gotten back together with her boyfriend David. David had been in our lives since I was about 12 years old. A few days after they first met, we all moved in together; me, my mom, David, and his three kids. Then my mom and I would move out, then back in. It was all very healthy. Their relationship hit a bit of a standstill when she threw a lamp at him and he responded with a restraining order. But, that was water under the bridge I suppose, as they got back together shortly after, albeit, long distance. He was living in Santa Barbara, while my mom and I were in NYC. I noticed that his visits to New York became more frequent, but again, I didn't like to ask questions unless they directly involved me. I just thought that he was super into my mom now that she started working out again. She had a pilates body from going to the gym five times a week for the past six months. Me, being entirely superficial, thought she was just trying to fit into her old skinny jeans but was actually trying to cure whatever it was that she had, through exercise and pressed juices.

At the end of my 10th grade school year, David and my mom took off for Paris one afternoon, I assumed they went to party. I was wrong. They traveled to Paris to get her official diagnosis from one of the doctors at the forefront of the disease. She stayed in Paris for the entire summer going from doctor visits to doctor visits, trying to hear some good news. The entire time she was gone, I was in the dark. I knew she was sick, but I didn't know that she was like *sick*, sick. But, I had this cloud in the back of my mind of the idea that my mom was going to die and it could be very soon. If I were being dramatic, I would say that summer was my limbo. I was halfway sure that nothing was wrong, but halfway sure that my mom had this funny little thing called ALS.

That summer, my grandparents on my mom's side were in charge, and it was quite miserable. It might have been the fact that I was forced to go on a family road trip from my home in New York to Charleston, or the lack of In-n-Out Burgers on the East Coast. But, I was allowed to be pissed. I had this lingering secret in the back of my mind. I wasn't as dumb as I looked, I knew something was wrong. Finally one night, I broke. I told my grandparents what I knew and they both didn't really say anything. They never were great with comforting unless it involved food. That's when I got on the phone with my mom and we finally had an honest conversation about what the fuck was going on. This was the only time I could tell that my mom was scared. This was the only conversation we had about ALS where we didn't make any jokes about it.

----

There's a photo series of prisoner's last meal requests before their death sentence. I imagine that I would have vodka fusilli pasta, a Nestle Toll House chocolate chip cookie, a 7-up and a side of Chick Fil A chicken nuggets. And maybe seconds. For some reason, the excitement of imagining having your dream meal, makes the death sentence not even that bad anymore. The thought of dying is overshadowed by the pure joy of tasting a warm chocolate chip cookie. This is how my mom dealt with her death sentence.

My mom, Ellie, was diagnosed with ALS at the age of 42. ALS stands for Amyotrophic Lateral Sclerosis, also known as Lou Gehrig's disease. I hope my legacy isn't for whatever rare disease I developed. I pray they don't name a new form of antiviral resistant strain of herpes after me once I die from it. ALS is a disease that isn't usually found in people under 60. It's also a disease that has no cure. It's not like AIDs though, you don't live with ALS; it kills you.

Here's the rundown on what ALS does to the human body. It's classified as a motor neuron disease, killing the neurons in your brain that send signals to your muscles to move. Your voluntary muscles are dead when this happens. This leads to paralysis of not only your limbs, but all your muscles, impacting your breathing and your speaking, too. You can also get bed sores.

Here's the kicker: nobody knows how you get this disease, you kinda just do. There are some theories about it being caused by being slim or from sports, but that's about it. That's why I have dedicated myself to being overweight and lazy. Once you are told that you have ALS, which is a lengthy process in itself, you are also told that all of this will happen very soon and to get your affairs in order, cause you got like two years to live. First of all, what the fuck? Why hasn't anyone found the cure for this disease? Were they too busy focusing on erectile dysfunction to solve this one? Probably. Thanks Viagra.

Within a year, you lose your ability to walk and use your arms. Essentially, you become just a head. And in my mom's case, a really bossy head with a blowout. Her diagnosis at 42 was extremely rare, but it happens. Still, why was this happening to us? She once said was thankful for the fact that she's even had 42 years of life. That's because she's a positive person, but I was not. Can you imagine having your body just shut down on you when you're only 42? I cannot imagine a worse disease, even Ebola has a treatment plan.

My whole life, it had always been just me and my mom, no offense to anyone. I had a dad obviously, but they were never married or even a couple, word on the street is that I was the product of a one night stand. She had gotten married to my stepdad, John, when I was a year old, but they split up ten years later. Then David had entered the picture, but no one thought that would last, even though it did. It was just me and my mom, in it together. We were a team, so why was one of our players being benched only halfway through the game? I'm not even sure if that sport analogy made sense; I never played any to know the correct terms.

The worst part about ALS is that you never lose any of your brain function. You stay totally lucid the entire time. Yes, you are completely aware of what is happening to you, that you are trapped in a dead body and you know that there isn't any hope coming your way EVER. With cancer, you get a chance. It might not be a good chance, but it's there. With ALS, however, the most hope that you are given is a prescribed drug that might extend your life by three months, MIGHT being the keyword. Everyone is fucking clueless about this disease.

So my mom was given her death sentence, but she kept getting a retrial. She passed the two year mark, then the third, then the fourth, fifth and so on. She was a medical anomaly if I do say so myself. I fully believe that she managed to outsmart the doctors because of her head on approach to tackling her disease. She didn't sit back and just wait to die like she was told. She decided that this was going to be her time to really live life to the fullest, no holding back. She also knew she needed to live for me. She was going to stretch out her time as long as she could. She wasn't supposed to last as long as she did and when she was told she couldn't do something, she pouted and gave you the silent treatment until she could.

Because ALS is so rare and also really fucking gross, it's not talked about much, not even between ALS patients. When my mom received her diagnosis, she went to a support group, in hopes of learning about what she was in for. She wanted to hear the stories of other patients and what their day to day was like. But, instead, she became depressed and left. Everyone at this meeting was sulking and talking about their fears. They had every right to do so, after all, ALS is scary, but this was not the path my mom wanted to follow. She would have lost her mind if she did it this way. Instead, she came home from the meeting that day with a new outlook.

"Look, all of this really fucking sucks," she told me. "If you want to scream, scream. If you want to cry, cry. If you want to blame it on me, then blame me. Let's get all of this out right now, because I'm not going to live like that. If you want to do this my way, you can and if you don't you're grounded." She was holding my hand as she said this.

She was fully aware that this affected me as much as it affected her. That it wasn't fair that this was happening and someone to blame it on would be nice. So we sat there that day and cried together. We got it all out at this moment. I was angry at the world for giving my mom this sentence. Why me? Why her? I was fearful of what was going to happen and fearful for the future. The moment I learned of my mom's ALS, I became a different person. My mom used to talk about ALS stealing my innocence, but that made it sound like ALS took my virginity so I wouldn't say it that way. However, ALS took my spirit. I am forever plagued with the memories that ALS gave us. I started to look at life a little differently, realizing that nothing is forever, not even a diamond, like they would like to convince you. But, it seems like that show Grey's Anatomy might make it to forever.

After we got all of this out, we made some decisions about how we were going to handle this: with dignity and grace. Just kidding, we were going to laugh at death in the face and not take it seriously for as long as we could and I was going to remind her that she still needed to wax. If we could joke about it, things would be better. We both knew the outcome of this disease, so why be all serious about it? The final six years of my mom's life were filled with laughing, cashmere, high carb foods, tears, and swearing. As much as we tried to always turn ALS into a joke, there are certain moments that are just not possible.

Like when you realize that your mother will never be able to hug you back. That wasn't funny. I still remember the last hug that I got from my mom, that didn't involve me lifting her arms onto my shoulders. You don't even realize that one day, that will be your last hug from your mother. It's just something that you realize over time and makes you wish that you really savored the one that was the last. Or, having to say our goodbyes, multiple times, was not funny. Something that you do know might be your last, is when there's a goodbye. Surgery became a common occurrence during this period, and with each surgery comes the risk that saying your goodbyes at the end of the hallway, could be the last time. But, what was funny was when she fell off the toilet, we laughed about that.

One of the unmentioned side effects of ALS is a desensitivity towards nudity. I have seen my mother naked much more than anyone should ever see anyone naked. She liked to rub this in by singing "Welcome to the Jungle" anytime she was pantless and motion towards her bush. Nudity is now funny to me and I find that actually showing you ass when mooning someone to not only be the proper method, but rude not to. Side note, mooning someone is hilarious and is best when done at a chain restaurant, like a Buffalo Wild Wings.

On August 31, 2016, my mother ended her life. She wanted me to say it this way so it sounded like suicide rather than losing a battle with her disease. Anything is more glamorous than ALS. And my mom loved glamour, that's probably why she loved the Bravo channel but more about that later.

The experience of growing up surrounded by death and disease (to be dramatic) made me a complete softy. I used to never cry in movies or at anything that anyone else would consider "sad," but now I cry all the time. I wasn't very empathetic, because nothing really bad has ever happened to me and I wasn't able to relate. But, after my mom passed, everything I had been through sunk in. I feel like I can relate to the pain of others. Ok, maybe I should rephrase that because I'm coming off like a serial killer who found Jesus. I'm just trying to say that I am a big baby anytime something sappy or sad happens.

Let's get to the funny stuff because now I'm crying. Thank God I'm not in public.

The Mosque in Paris, 14 years apart.

## All Brats Go To Paris

For a brief moment in time, specifically 1995-2007, I believed I was going to be a star. I did not have any acting ability, couldn't sing and didn't have a comprehensive reform policy. I was planning on marrying Justin Bieber, cementing my status as A-list and eventually starting my own clothing line that specializes in plastic tube tops. I didn't know how I would achieve this goal, but my unwavering confidence convinced me that I had what it takes to make the face of Proactiv fall in love with me. I possessed the confidence to wear basketball shorts over tights proudly. I was able to walk in my fourth grade classroom, sit at the front of the room and compliment the teachers smock dress. I tried out for the lead of Dorothy in the sixth grade production of The Wizard of Oz, where I auditioned with 'Somewhere Over The Rainbow' in front of the entire grade. I did not get the part, but I didn't even care. I was a machine, unstoppable by other people's thoughts and judgment. I knew I was special and I was dead set on showing everyone that.

Then, middle school hits and everything sucks. I became hyper-aware of my body and my voice and my words. It wasn't an overnight occurrence either, it was a slow decline into major social anxiety and a debilitating spray tan addiction.

I forgot my sweat pants for gym class one day and was forced to wear the basketball uniform shorts from the lost in found. The thought of who's sweaty basketball shorts these were did not phase me. I changed in the bathroom and ran down the track to meet up with the rest of the class.

"Wow, do you live on the moon?" One boy asked pointing at my obscenely pale legs.

His clever yet hurtful comment was only the first of many.

"Is this your first time outside?"

"I see why you always wear pants." This one didn't sting too much, I was almost happy that someone noticed what I wore regularly.

One girl even put on her sunglasses, "Your legs are burning my eyes."

I walked up to the gym teacher and asked her, "Can I go back inside, I don't feel very good."

I thought that since she was a woman, she would have some sympathy for me and my varicose vein legs, but she didn't, "You're going to need a note from a doctor to skip class. Go line up."

I walked away and whispered "dyke" under my breath. I had just learned this term and thought it was a real stinger. I lined up with all the tan girls, ready to run this mile as fast as I could so I could go back inside and get back into the comfort of my jeans.

It took me twelve minutes to run that mile, almost double the time of the other kids. They all sat on the bench and watched a ghost run circles in the dirt. I went home after school that day and had my mom sign me up for "independent gym." The rest of the year I would turn in a sheet of paper with my mom's signature saying I went to tennis lessons twice a week. I did not go to tennis lessons.

Later that year, we had a mid-semester class beach party. I had already forgotten all about the devastation my pale legs caused my classmates and was excited to go swimming with all my friends. I bought a cute new tankini from the Gap and counted down the days. My mom had been letting me use her self tan lotion so I could avoid future embarrassment. She sympathized with my desire to be tan, we were living in Southern California. What she didn't do is tell me how to apply it. I slathered it on my legs, just my legs. I heard you weren't supposed to tan your feet, so I stopped at the ankle. And because no one teased me about my pale arms, I assumed they weren't a problem. I stripped down to my bathing suit at the beach and ran towards the ocean. My legs had a strange yellow/orange glow to them while the rest of my body resembled that of a corpse. I would soon learn from a Cosmopolitan quiz that I have blue undertones. After getting out of the ocean, I quickly toweled off, exfoliating any of the fake tan that hadn't been washed away from the saltwater. I was now just as pale as before, and this time there were photos to prove it.

The next day at school, everyone gathered around the projection screen in the computer room and looked at the photos from the party. I was holding my breath that there wouldn't be any of me, but luck was not on my side.

"She looks like an oreo!" a boy shouted when a photo of me popped up.

He wasn't wrong, so I said nothing. I also couldn't think of a witty retort. The photo captured me on my way back from the bathroom. I had slipped on my black converse and my black sweatshirt but skipped pants. My bare legs looked like the white cream filling sandwiched between two black cookies.

For some reason, no adult picked up on this and considered it bullying. I wasn't getting body slammed into a locker or my underwear wasn't being pulled up and over my head, but I was being bullied and no one was doing anything to stop it. I was being made fun of something I couldn't change. I skipped the next beach party.

8th grade graduation was coming up and I had bought a black mini dress from the clubwear store BeBe. I had seen a girl wearing it in Seventeen Magazine and immediately knew that it was the dress for me, and it was under my $100 budget. But, it was a short dress and therefore, my legs would be on display. I started discussing my options with my mom. I suggested illegal tanning pills from the dark web, she suggested a place called Mystic Tan. This was before airbrush tanning had been invented, so it was an automatic booth that would spray you head to toe.

The day before graduation, my mom picked me up from school and took me to the mall.

"When you get in there, it'll tell you to turn around so it can spray your back. Don't do that though, stay twice on the front and then twice for the back. It'll be darker this way." She told me from her own experience, and she always looked evenly tanned after using this machine, so I trusted her.

I didn't factor in the fact that she was much tanner naturally than I was. Being butt ass white makes for a difficult natural spray tan and I can easily look like someone with vitiligo.

"Do you have an appointment?" The woman behind the counter asked. She was the color of bacon and smelled like it too. This place also had tanning beds that I'm now thankful I wasn't allowed to use.

"Yes, it's for my daughter." My mom said looking at me. The appointment obviously was for me, I was almost see through. "Grace O'Connell."

I punched my mom on her right butt cheek, I clearly had stated earlier to use a pseudonym.

"Ok, follow me." She said and handed me a small heart sticker. "You can put this somewhere like your stomach or your arm so you'll have a little heart tattoo when you get out and then you can see how much darker you are than before."

"Why would I want to do that?" I asked as I put the sticker in my pocket.

She opened the door to a small room with a spaceship inside. My new white Nikes stuck to the floor as I walked in.

"You're going to want to undress completely, put your hair up in a hairnet, apply lotion to your hands and feet so they don't get any of the formula on them and towel off lightly when you're done." She handed me the small white towel and closed the door on her way out.

I was on my own now. I undressed and stared at my small yet chunky body in the full length mirror. I looked like a blueberry, but that was a battle for another day. I put my hair into the hair net and grabbed a second one to put over my face. I didn't want to look like the receptionist, I thought it would look more normal if my face was a little lighter than my body. I decided to skip the lotion step because of my previous misstep with not tanning my feet. I was planning on wearing sandals to graduation and didn't want to look like I was also wearing white ankle socks with them. I deemed myself ready and stepped into the booth. I hit the start button and then disobeyed the machine's instructions. I didn't turn around, I did a double whammy for the front, hit the start button again and turned around.

The transformation was complete, I stepped out of the booth and checked myself out.

"Uh oh," I said as I saw my new race in the mirror.

Brown liquid was now dripping off my body into puddles. I quickly reached for the towel and tried to wipe it all off. The rough towel was taking off the freshly applied tan in patches. I looked like Micheal Jackson. I kept on scrubbing until I was the color of a Neapolitan ice cream bar. Panic and embarrassment set in when I looked at myself a final time in the mirror.

*Who let me in here alone?* I thought. *I'm only a child.*

I quickly got dressed back into my jeans and white t-shirt and walked out. I was unaware that I would end up with the imprint of my jeans on my freshly dyed legs.

"Don't worry, it's going to look great, it just takes a few hours to settle." My mom was always one to downplay a situation. She knew it looked awful, but she couldn't let me know. "We can just apply some tanning lotion on top when we get home, it'll even everything out."

Her intentions were in the right place, but she was wrong. I had stopped taking her beauty advice years earlier when I got a bad haircut and she suggested I cut it all off into a pixie. We got as far as the hair salon styling my bob into a Kris Jenner shag before I realized that one of my ears is much larger than my other and that I can never have a hair cut above my shoulders.

Instead of following her advice, I went to the internet to try to find a solution to a splotchy yet dark fake tan. I tried all the methods, baking soda, lemon juice, a hot bath, nothing seemed to work, I just was irritating it. This tan had a mind of its own, and it was angry. I went to bed hoping for a miracle in the morning.

When I woke up, I found that the color was not that bad, I looked like I had spent a few days on a tropical island, nothing crazy. It was the patchiness that was bad. My knees were on different tropical vacation than I was and were the color of mahogany. My feet were not sandal ready. And there was a line right under my chin that mimicked where two oceans meet. Graduation was two hours away and I decided I wasn't going.

"You are going to your graduation, don't be a dumbass. There is no way in hell I'm missing this moment." My mom yelled as she tried zipped up my dress. "No one will even notice the streaks, it's better than being pale right?"

She had a point. I stopped pushing out my stomach to the 6 month mark and let her zip up the dress completely.

My mom was wrong, she didn't know how clever and cruel 8th grade girls could be. Everyone commented on my bad tan, this was worse than being pale. Now people knew that their insistent bullying got to me and I tried to change myself for them.

After the ceremony, I opted out of the party in favor of going home and eating a bowl of cereal in bed.

"Mommy, I don't think I want to go to this school next year."

"Well, that's good because we're moving to Paris."

This was not an odd remark coming from my mom, it was as normal as her telling me we were having spaghetti for dinner. I brushed off this comment and continued updating my Facebook status to Gracie O'Connell is: it's raining. This wasn't a metaphor for the emotional hardship another move would take on me, it was actually raining and I was new to social media. Moving to an entirely new city was something I had done four times already and I hadn't even started high school yet. This time, the move didn't sound that bad. Santa Barbara had run its course and it was time I tricked everyone into thinking I was bilingual.

The only thing that really stressed me out about this move, if the move was actually happening, was French teenagers. In my mom's eyes, I was the hippest and coolest girl to be around. She was right, but other kids didn't see that yet. The kids in Santa Barbara didn't care if I had been in the newspaper three times or that I had grown out of my lactose intolerance without any medical assistance. And if they didn't care, French teenagers certainly wouldn't care. There is nothing more terrifying than French teenagers. I had witnessed them first hand on a trip to Paris in the 5th grade. They traveled in groups of four and always took up the entire sidewalk. The boys were fond of wearing fur-trimmed puffer coats and didn't mind demanding a stranger to bum them a cigarette. The girls looked like they had only survived on human growth hormone laced milk and MDMA. 3 pm was a frightening time in France as they bombarded the metro after school got out.

I didn't believe that I could handle going to school in a different country, my legs looked awful in capris and I didn't know how to smoke cigarettes. I had tried smoking a Pixi Stix as practice but it didn't work and I think it gave me the black lung.

I opened up my laptop and began researching options for high school in Paris. I came across the American School of Paris which looked promising. I began to envision myself walking down the hallways with my new Hannah Montana haircut and a belly full of baguette. The kids in my daydream began to make me say French words with my American accent and I snapped out of it. I couldn't do this, I had to let my mom know that I was going to stay behind and live on my own in Santa Barbara.

"I don't think you understand how mean everyone looked in the photos for the school," I said pulling up the webpage of three teenagers of all different races smiling.

"They look nice, she would be your friend!" My mom said as she clicked around the website.

"These people won't get me, I'm just going to have to stay here and maintain the property."

"This is a rental."

"Well then I'll go live with Madison and we can go to school together." Madison was my best friend and her mom bought the best snacks.

"You are not going to stay with Madison for the rest of your life. You're coming to Paris with me because I am your family. You can have a say as to what school you attend but chose fast, you only have a few months before class starts."

"I don't want to go to school there, everyone is already going to know each other and there won't be any room for me at the lunch table!"

"I can come and pick you up for lunch if you want."

"That's not an option!"

I stormed back to my room, opened my laptop and Googled emancipation. I contemplated throwing myself down the stairs and telling a child protective service agent that my mom did it. I began to stretch in preparation for my beat up when an add came across the TV for an online school. I stopped what I was doing and researched this K12 program.

K12 was an online school that you could do from anywhere in the world. It seemed legit but I also did not have the best judgment. Earlier in the day, I had used my mom's social security number in an attempt to win an iPhone 4. I started looking at the course options and for the first time, I was excited. I would have a choice as to what science class, what art class, even what math class I could take. I had never taken an active interest in my schooling because the entire time I was just paranoid that the teacher would call on me when I didn't raise my hand. This would instantly solve that problem, since I would be the only kid in the class.

I immediately began making a powerpoint as to why I should be homeschooled. I had learned how to use powerpoint the year prior and had started using it every time I needed to make a point. The last one on why we should implement Taco Tuesday not only on Tuesday but also on Thursday was a real homerun.

A few hours later, I called my mom to my room to show her my carefully laid out argument.

"I firmly believe that I am not built for a regular high school, especially one where alcohol will be served to minors. You don't want me to become an alcoholic do you?" I began the powerpoint. "But you see, we have options that are on the cutting edge of technology. I present to you online high school."

My mom looked intrigued as I made my points, the main one being that it would free her up from the restraints of only traveling on school holidays. With my high school being online, we would be able to move freely and whenever she wished. I pointed out the art history class I could take, where I would then be able to go and see what I was studying in person, rather than from a screen. The smile on her face indicated that she was sold.

"Now, let me bring you to slide 12," I said using my laser pointer.

"You don't need to, I think this is a great idea. Let's do it. Good job." She leaned over and began to investigate the website on my laptop.

I panicked. I hated when she used my laptop, I knew she would go through my search history and know that I looked up emancipation. She once borrowed my computer to watch a movie and I erased the entire Safari app in an effort to prevent her from seeing that I searched "how to kiss good."

"Let's do that later, why don't we celebrate with some tuna fish sandwiches?" I said closing my computer.

One month later, we were on a flight to Paris. My grandma would be meeting us there a day later. My mom bought us business class tickets at my grandma's expense and she didn't want her to find out, so she had her fly alone.

Even though I got my way with homeschooling and was sitting in a plush business class lounger, I still wasn't happy. I didn't want to start all over again, Santa Barbara was home and we were abandoning it in favor of a city that I wasn't too sure wanted us.

My mom and David had just broken up for the tenth time and I could tell that it was one of the main factors of us moving across the ocean. I get my flair for the dramatics from my mom obviously. The breakup didn't last long though because soon they were chatting on the phone every other day. Her plan of showing him how unattainable, spontaneous and how much she loved cheese worked.

We had now been in Paris for a month and tensions were running high between my mom and grandma. They would fight to the point that police would have to be called in for reinforcement one moment and be making lunch plans the next. The main reason for their fighting was simply because my grandma would embarrass my mom in public.

One day my grandma was in line at an office supply store and a sweet old French woman politely asked her if she was in line, "Etes-Vous en linge?"

"I'm an American." My grandma replied with two rolls of bubble wrap under her arms.

No shit she was American. My mom walked out of the store and took up smoking. I was always put in the middle of choosing whose side I was on. Legally, I was on my mom's side, but my grandma made me chicken piccata anytime I asked. I was torn. But this time I stayed inside the store with my grandma because she had told me she would buy me the pack of highlighters I wanted.

The day after, my mom took me on a walk around the Seine after lunch. We were living in the 7th arrondissement at the moment, a short walk from the Louvre. She decided we would pop in and check out a new exhibit she had wanted to see. On our way, we passed my favorite block that was comprised of five different pet shops.

"Can we go in and just look?" I asked with a diabolical look in my eye. I knew my mom wouldn't be able to resist a French bulldog puppy that I had decided just then that I needed.

Immediately I spotted him. His body resembled a potato with ears, he was white with a few black spots and had the face that said "help me." I poked my mom's thigh and pointed him out. We both got on our knees to check him out more. He came over to the window of his cage while his siblings continued to sleep. I put my finger through the crack and he licked it. His breath smelled like the best eau de toilette money could buy.

"You told me we could get a dog, remember? You said that I could get one." I said trying to rack my brain for if she had ever said that. We had plenty of dogs but they usually weren't premeditated. They were either gifted to me by a family friend or gave me a look that said take me home with you, and I complied.

"He is super cute," she said looking for someone to help us get a closer look at him. "You'd have to take him on walks every day."

I nodded my head that I would. I wouldn't.

45 minutes later we left the pet store with a French bulldog puppy named Leo. I was in love, deep in love. The type of love that could cause me to commit murder-suicide if anyone ever threatened to take him away. We walked back to our apartment as I clutched him in my arms. I was never going to let his precious feet hit the pavement.

The next few weeks were hell. The little angel I had carried home from the pet shop had abandoned his body and let satan take over. He was sneaky like satan too. When he jumped onto the coffee table and stole my retainer off my plate, it took me 30 minutes to find. He had buried it in the planter on the balcony. He enjoyed eating shoes that he knew I had just bought. He also suffered from irritable bowel syndrome. It might have been from all the brie I fed him but I wasn't going to take away his favorite food just because it gave him diarrhea.

Since he couldn't be left alone in the apartment and my grandma refused to babysit her great-grandson, he went everywhere with me. I had bought a large purse like Paris Hilton and had him ride in it all around town. When my arm would hurt, I would pull him out of the bag and hand him over to my mom. Even though she threatened to throw him off the Eiffel tower I knew she loved having him because she would use him as an excuse to go outside and have a cigarette. Also, he had the squishiest face.

We hit the two month mark of living in Paris and it was time I started school so I didn't end up as a cast member of Teen Mom. I set up my desk perfectly with color-coordinated binders and bowls of snacks for my self proclaimed recess. By noon that day, I was done with my work.

Since my only friend in the country was my mom, I spent the rest of my days following her around cockblocking her at cafes. She once was asked on a date by Adrien Brody when I was in the bathroom. Upon my arrival back to the table, he backed out, clearly not ready to be a step-father.

The loneliness of living in Paris was getting to us. Since none of us had visas, we were required to leave the European Union every three months in order to reset our visas. London was only a 2 hour train away and outside of the union. This little trick would later allow me to attend four years of college in France without ever applying for a visa. I later learned that this was not true and not an effective way of avoiding deportation. My mom called her friend Susan who agreed to meet us in London with her daughter, my friend Sarah.

My mom broke the news to my grandma that she wasn't invited. Looking back at my mom's behavior to my grandma breaks my heart, but then I realized that I would do the same to my mom if given the opportunity. It's just a fact that daughters don't enjoy spending time with their mothers even when they choose to spend all their time together.

Our weekend in London opened my eyes to just how cool my mom actually was. I didn't want to do things without her, I wouldn't even know what to do except hang out at Build-A- Bear and get lost in grocery stores. She had never even been to London before this and somehow knew all the secret spots and even got us into Annabelle's private club by flirting with the bouncer and dropping Randy Jackson's name.

Everything came naturally to her, especially making friends. This is something that was not passed down to me, it must skip a generation because my grandma's only friend is her trainer. I don't make friends easily, I don't know how to participate in small talk that isn't about me and I don't enjoy meeting up with people outside my home. My mom could meet someone and be invited to spend the summer on their boat in Ibiza in the same night. I realized I actually liked my mom, I knew I loved her, but this was the first time I actually liked her. I felt bad for praying that she would get hit by a car because she wouldn't let me wear a Von Dutch hat that said Von Bitch.

It was obvious that I was spending too much time with my dog Leo. I was caught having a one-sided argument with him over who was a better dancer, Paula Abdul or Patrick Swayze, and we came to the conclusion that I needed to hang out with someone my own age and species. My mom decided that we would bring my friend Sarah back to Paris with us for however long she was comfortable being away from home. Sarah was born a grown-up, when my mom asked her if she would like to come back to Paris with us she replied, "Yeah, I'll go ahead and book my mom a flight home." It wouldn't be surprising if she got her own apartment across the hall during her visit. Sarah was also homeschooled so she could live in Paris with me indefinitely.

While Sarah was waiting for her lease application to go through, we spent our days doing "8 minute abs" workouts in the living room while my mom and grandma fought. One day they fought for 45 minutes about stale bread. After the dust settled, my mom took Sarah, Leo and I to blow off steam at Zara.

There was an end of the summer sale on rhinestone encrusted tank tops that would require two hands to filter through. Earlier that day Leo had eaten an entire bag of mini saucissons that I left out and I could feel his sweet little belly now rumbling in regretful satisfaction. I handed Leo over to my mom.

"What did you feed him?" She asked holding him at an arms length.

"He had a little charcuterie for breakfast." Leo was too good for dog food, he was French.

My mom set Leo down on the marble floors and made her way to the 2 for 1 sunglasses section. Leo was refusing to walk like he always did, so he was just dragged over by his harness. As his butt shimmied across the cold ground, he left a trail of fresh poop behind him.

"Mom!" I yelled. "Leo!"

She turned around to witness the horror scene that was unfolding. A tagliatelle noodle was hanging out of him now, which was strange because Leo didn't even like Italian food. Sarah attempted to divert traffic while simultaneously not making direct eye contact with anyone. I pretended I didn't know any of them. My mom pulled a few napkins out of her purse and tried to clean up the mess, but ended up just spreading it around. I prayed she would pull a travel sized 401 spray out of her purse next.

"Gracie! Go get me some more tissues!" She shouted from the floor. The napkins she had in her purse had been used up already.

Leo wasn't going to stop unless he was corked. I looked in his carrier for a wee-wee pad that could be fashioned into a diaper but came out empty handed. The only thing slightly resembling a towel was the cotton sweater I had tied around my waist. I threw it over to my mom and she began mopping the floor with it and a few squirts of hand sanitizer. Leo escaped his harness and excused himself to relieve himself near the shoe section. I ran over to him and picked him up before he was finished with his business.

"There's more over there." I pointed to the new mess that my mom would have to clean up.

Ever the creative, my mom walked over to a mannequin and pulled out the tissue paper that was being used to stuff the sleeves. She picked up the new dog poop and walked out of the store. Sarah and I followed with Leo now in his carrier.

"The dog never eats again." She said in a huff. She walked to the corner to try to hail a cab while Sarah and I just looked at each other. Her white t-shirt was now brown and her hair was matted to her forehead from sweat.

As my mom turned around to make sure we were following, she saw who she deemed "her first Frenchie." My mom had dated a man, or should I say, boy, named Arnaud. This was when I was in 3rd grade and before my mom ever met David. He was 20 years old and visiting America for the first time. He was movie star handsome and spoke in broken English. He moved into our house a week after their first dance at the club Wildcat. After two months of living with us, Arnaud moved back to Paris since his parents stopped sending him money. He broke up with my mom via email shortly after he arrived back in his home country. My mom was left broken hearted and taped a printed copy of his email on our fridge. She never spoke to him again until this moment.

"Ellie? Iz zat youh?" He asked in shock.

"No, it's not." She got into the cab and left Sarah, Leo and I in front of Zara. Don't worry, she circled the block and picked us up.

The next week, the fighting within the apartment got worse. A simple misplaced fork could blow my mom's temper off. One particular blowout fight resulted in my mom and I abandoning Paris altogether. Sarah, Leo, my mom and I packed up our belongings and headed to the airport. Leo expressed his concerns that he wouldn't have the same quality of life he was used to in Paris, but was reassured when he found out that we would be going to my mom's friend Diandra's $60 million dollar home in Spain. Sarah boarded a flight back to Los Angeles without any unaccompanied minor paperwork, she was above that. My mom, Leo and I hustled to make our one way flight to the island of Mallorca.

And just like that, Paris was dead. We abandoned both my grandma and the dream in favor of a new plan. We were going to go to Mallorca so my mom could "clear her head" then start a new life. I was convinced we were joining witness protection.

The entire two months we "lived" in Paris, I had a gut feeling that we would be returning to the states come Fall. The signs were pretty obvious, obvious enough that a 14 year old could tell that there was no long term plan to become expats, just wishful thinking. I later learned that the reason we didn't end up staying in Paris was not because my mom and grandma couldn't fathom being roommates anymore, it was because they ran out of money. And my 300€ a month crepe habit wasn't helping, nor was the 2000€ dog with the 150€ collar. We were literally living on a prayer.

Diandra and my mom came up with the game plan for my mom to create a life that was no longer dependent on an allowance from my grandpa. For most of my mom's adult life, she survived on the generosity of my grandpa. No one really understood what he did for a living, but no one complained when he would send us to Hawaii for 2 week stays.

The plan was to move back to Santa Barbara and my mom would work on selling Diandra's house, then move to NYC and start over there. Diandra had a property in every time zone. The Santa Barbara house was a beautiful Spanish style retreat up high in the hills. There was a zen garden, tennis court, ocean view, and 20 million dollar price tag. Opera ended up purchasing the house. HAHA

With the uncertainty of the upcoming move presented, I opted to continue homeschooling. I had gotten accustomed to the leisurely mornings and 3 hour work days, I wasn't about to trade that in for eating my lunch in a bathroom stall. I was given the choice and I believe I made the right one. I often get criticized by people for missing out on the high school experience, as if my not going to prom affected their life in some way. I'm happy I don't ever have to go to a high school reunion and get tricked into joining a pyramid scheme.

8th grade graduation.

# Balensheaga

When I turned 10 years old, I wrote on my birthday wishlist "Chanel Markers" Since the moment I was born, I was under the impression that I deserved designer goods, that I was fabulous. I was an only child, so my only sense of the world was through my mom's eyes and the places she took me. From my eye level, all I saw were nice purses. Everywhere we went, everyone had a designer bag. And I had a Jansport backpack filled with old oranges from yesterday's lunch.

When we moved to New York, my cravings for luxury goods got even worse. Gossip Girl had just aired and I wanted to be Serena Van Der Woodson more than I wanted air. I already lived in New York, I went to adult dinner parties, I was halfway there (I thought). I just needed the wardrobe. I had already started hitting up discount shops for any Helmut Lang or Juicy Couture I could get my hands on. But, these discount stores did not have discount designer handbags, unless you count a Kate Spade. All the girls at my school carried either a Kate Spade purse or a look-alike from whatever corner store existed in Queens. I wanted to walk in and really show them. I was campaigning for queen bee. This was also my first (and only) go at high school. I hadn't learned that the queen bee role was something just in movies and tv shows. I also do not have the personality for queen bee, I am all talk and cower at the first thought of confrontation.

I had heard stories about a magical place called Canal Street. This was in 2010 so the government hadn't been able to crack the whip on counterfeit goods yet, to my pleasure. I knew I wouldn't be allowed to go to Chinatown to buy knock offs alone though, so I had to get my mom to agree to go with me. It wasn't that hard.

Over Cheerios one morning, I brought it up, "Mommy, do you think you can take me downtown to Soho this weekend?" I figured Soho sounded better than Chinatown.

"Maybe, why?" She asked while taking a sip of her coffee that was 90% half and half.

"Well, there's this place I read about and it's where everyone goes to get fake bags and jewelry," I said trying to make it sound casual.

"Is it a store or what is it?" She questioned. I clearly piqued her interest.

"Well, kinda. I don't really know but they're supposed to have everything, but it's all cheap and fake. But really good fakes."

"What time do they open?" She asked wide eyed and bushy tailed.

"Well, they don't exactly have store hours. It's kinda like a flea market, but for fake products, so it's kept on the down low." I said informing her with the little research I had done. I thought Canal street was one of New York's best kept secrets, mainly because I only just heard about it.

If you're not familiar with Canal Street, I feel bad for you. It doesn't exist to the degree it used to exist though. Obama got involved and started to crack down on counterfeit goods being sold in America. Now they only sell bags with blatant misspellings like "Door" for "Dior" and "Fucci" for "Gucci". But, in 2010, you could get the real fake deal.

Canal Street was the name of the actual street the dealers were on.

There were some storefronts on the actual store with Samsung phone cases and I heart NY shirts on display. You had to go in and ask if they had anything designer. The salespeople were usually either 105 or 12, something about this job being the lowest on the totem pole. Their middle age counterparts got to sit on a ladder in the back, supervising and smoking clove cigarettes. Once they heard you use the word designer, they lifted up the table's skirt and brought out a black trash bag filled with Chanel, Fendi and Louis Vuitton. These replicas were pretty good. They had all the spelling correct but if you got too close, your breath would evaporate the "leather."

"Eh, how much for this one?" My mom asked pointing to a classic Chanel flap bag inside the trash bag.

"50 dollar." She replied while keeping her eyes on the street for anyone who looked suspicious.

"I don't know, it looks a little plasticky." She replied, running her hand against the pleather.

It did, all of the bags in the trash bag looked a little plastic. But, what were we expecting from a trash bag? We walked away defeated but still optimistic that this particular stand was just the worst one here, and the best was yet to come. I like to think of myself as a glass half full kinda gal. I always envision the best of any situation. While, most of the time, this keeps me smiling and looking forward to the future, other times it leaves me disappointed, like this time. We had been to numerous stands and they all had the same exact bad fakes.

"Do you want to go grab lunch?" My mom asked me, trying to avoid any more disappointment.

"Yeah, I guess so," I said with a frown. I had such high hopes for this place. I did a full 15 minutes of research, I thought I would come in and breezily come out no longer resembling a middle class tween but rather a lady of leisure.

Just as we were walking back to the real Soho, we started hearing mumblings. A chant almost, "Chanel. Gucci. Prada" We didn't know where it was coming from. "Chanel. Gucci. Prada" Was this God himself, speaking to me, just a small town girl? Living in a lonely world? No, it was a small Chinese man whispering sweet nothings into my ear as I walked by.

"Where?" I asked and stopped us in our tracks.

"Follow me." He said grabbing both our arms.

I think the mixture of him being very petite, me being disappointed and the prospect of a fake Rolex, made my mom accept. She was the last person to follow anyone anywhere. She was the type of woman to immediately call the police if someone behind her took two of the same turns. She was hyper aware and hyper scared of everyone. I don't know what made her turn out this way, but she passed it onto me as well, so it might be genetic. I'm always worried I'm going to get kidnapped and sold into sex slavery. So was my mom actually, but I think she was just being vain. People with vaginas already ruined by children don't usually create a high demand in the sex trade market and she had yet to understand that. They wanted fresh meat.

So off we went. We followed him through the crowds, all holding hands. That might have been the strangest part actually. We arrived at his booth that looked identical to all the other booths we had spent the last few hours rejecting

"No we don't want these bags, we want the real bags." My mom said trying to be subtle about the poor craftsmanship she had been seeing.

"No no, follow me" He was a man of few words.

We obliged and followed him to the back of the shop and through the door frame covered by a blue tarp and onto the loading dock at the back. This was all seeming very Mission Impossible. We just wanted some purses. There were about six other people waiting outside as well, either lost or looking for some fakes. A van pulled up and we were instructed to get in. I had read about this online and knew it was part of the protocol. The dealers didn't keep their best stuff on the street anymore. Even though I knew that people have traveled this same journey before and survived, I got hesitant.

"What do you think?" I asked my mom quietly while we began to get hurdled with a few other mother daughter pairs. "Can we go?"

"There's no fucking way we're getting into that van." She replied and began to approach the driver. "Can you just tell me where to go? My daughter and I are just going to walk to wherever you're going."

"I can't give you an address." He said while glancing at the benches in the van filling up. The last row was now full.

"Perhaps this will persuade you." She said slyly passing him a 20 dollar bill. " You can just give me directions on where you're going. You can trust me, I'm not a narc."

He took the bait. "Go back to Canal, three blocks up then right, then 2 more blocks. Go to the back alley and wait."

We stood back and watched the van fill with cigarette smoke and the top 20 on 20 station before pulling away. My mom shot me a look that said "I'm making you watch Taken again after this" and pulled me alongside her.

We walked back through the store and onto Canal street. We were 1 block up Canal and only 5 minutes into our journey. My mom was walking as if her shoes had rails keeping her attached to the sidewalk. She didn't take steps, she just dragged her Converse on the cement.

"We gotta walk faster, the other people are going to get all the best stuff!" I said trying to pull her along.

"I can't walk any faster!" She shouted and stopped in the middle of the crowd. "I'm too tired, we're just going to have to do this another day."

"No, we can't! I need to get the stuff today, you promised me we could go today." I begged.

And so we kept walking. It took us 20 minutes to walk 5 blocks. My mom was sweating by the time we got there. She didn't want to disappoint me, no matter how stupid the request. At this point, she was sixth months away from getting her diagnosis. Her walking had slowed down, her hands always felt heavy. She used to call me into the bathroom and have me help her wash the conditioner out of her hair. But, still, none of this led me to believe that she couldn't just push through.

When we finally arrived at the back alley, all her instincts told her not to go into this warehouse. Some of my instincts told me that too, but I told them to shut up. A man opened a garage door on a loading dock and we followed him up the three flights of stairs and into a room.

The room itself was shabby, it was about the size of a gas station convenience store and had the same scent, hot dog air. But, instead of hot cheetos and slushies, there were the best luxury items a little bit of money could buy you. Most of the floor was covered in black tarps, to protect the merchandise from the floor. The bags were stacked in piles of corresponding styles. A stack of clutches, a stack of cross body's, a stack of hobos, etc. I personally would have preferred them to be organized by brand, because I'm pretty sure me and everyone else there were not just window shopping, but had a curated list in our minds of what to buy. You don't get in a stranger's van if you don't already know what you want. Or in our case, walk with a debilitating case of ALS in Chinatown.

My mom has never really been a purse person. She was low maintenance and would just use a Trader Joe's tote if she needed to bring more than 3 items with her. David bought her a Valentino purse once and she immediately gave it to me. Sorry David! She was just along for the knock off jewelry and accessories she could get. I on the other hand, love purses, I love bringing things with me. I don't bring cute things with me, like a little mirror or lip gloss, nothing that resembles an Us Weekly's 'What's in my bag' blurb. I never leave home without every key of every place I've ever entered, loose tic tacs, a decorative piglet figurine that I found on the floor, fake blood, Chick Fil A sauce packets and fourteen different chapsticks. I'm just an easy going girl like that.

Along with the purses, there was luggage and shoes and accessories. The store (is it a store?) had a dedicated jewelry section as well. It looked like the trunk of a rapper's Lamborghini, I wouldn't be surprised if this place also sold firearms. The diamonds were fake but they were real enough to me. Even at 15 I wanted a Cartier Love bracelet.

Now, I can't tell you exactly what we bought for the fear that an investigation may be opened if this book falls into the wrong hands. I don't want my Hermes clutch seized. Oops!

After the thrill of completing our purchase and learning some keywords in Mandarin, we were hooked. I understood the high of a junkie the moment I left that warehouse in lower Manhattan. I was clutching my goods in a "Thank you for Shopping" plastic bag and was sent out no longer a girl, but a woman. This was hardly the last time we ventured downtown. Now that we knew where this magical kingdom was, the middle man was cut out, we could make this trip everyday if we wanted!

The next weekend, we were back for more. This time, I wanted a cute little Chanel bag, the type club girls wear to trick their promoters into thinking they'll buy more than one cocktail. My mom decided she needed a Cartier watch in silver. The gold one she bought the previous week was already tarnishing. You get what you pay for, and here $30 got you a week.

My mom knew that she wouldn't last the walk or even a subway ride, so we cabbed it down to our new favorite place in the city. We waited outside until a van pulled up and went in with them. The stairs she climbed just a week ago now presented a problem. She physically couldn't get past the halfway mark. Nothing meant more to me at that moment than acquiring my purse, so put my shoulders under her butt, and pushed.

"Have you been working out?" She asked when we reached the top.

I shook my head no and wiped the sweat off my brow. I was really working for this purse. Was it even worth it? Yes! The following Friday I wore my cute new Chanel bag to a New Year's Eve party and got so many compliments!

I began to spiral out of control. Every day I thought of a new designer I wanted a piece of. "I just have to have the new Givenchy Pandora bag!" I shouted through our apartment.

And I got that Givenchy Pandora bag. My mom waited in the alley while I went up to make my purchase. The leather looked a little shinier than normal and I thought it might have said "Giverney," but I just attributed it to being dizzy from all the flights of stairs I had to climb and not having a second breakfast.

I took my new bag to school the following Monday, ready to impress Agnes, the only other girl in my grade who would know how special it was. She had mentioned to me before that it was sold out at both Saks and Barney's, which was the main reason I had to have it.

I sat down at my desk and placed my new purse on top for all the see and admire. Agnes finally walked into class and took her seat next to me, "Cute bag, how did you find one?"

"Oh, my aunt got it for me in Paris." I lied.

She picked up the bag and inspected it, "It says Giverny not Givenchy." She held it close to my face in triumph.

"That's how they spell it in France, it's an ode to Monet." I took the bag from her and held it tight in my lap. *Crap.*

"No they don't, this is fake. It's so obvious. Pathetic."

I sank down into my seat, avoiding eye contact with all the girls inching closer to get a better look to see if anything else about me was fake. I felt like a circus act and my at home highlights looked orange in this light. I was a clown. Why couldn't she just pass me a note that said my bag was fake, not out me in front of the whole class. I decided at that moment, I was done with high school and fake bags.

After class that day I hurried home to our apartment. I needed my mom to take me back to Canal Street to return the bag to get my $40 back or at least store credit.

"They don't take returns, it isn't Bloomingdales." My mom said when I pointed out the spelling mistake.

"Can we at least try?" I begged.

"I just don't think I can keep going all the way down there anymore, it's too much." She said.

"Oh, ok. I can just go by myself, it's fine." I compromised.

"No it's too dangerous, you have to go with an adult."

"You're my only adult though!" I sat down defeated. I was too scared to go alone honestly.

After that, I quit the high stakes fake it til you make it game, not by choice though. I couldn't find a guardian cool enough to go bag hunting with me like my mom was. No one was as cool as my mom was.

This was the first time ALS got in my way, got in her way. And she wasn't even diagnosed yet. This was the first time she wasn't able to do something because of her body. She used to pull me along on her adventures and put up with whatever tourist trap I wanted to participate in, and now, she was confined to the surrounding five blocks of the Upper East Side. A month later, she began her quest to figure out what the hell was wrong with her.

She got her first diagnosis and didn't tell me, and I didn't even notice. I was so distracted by her offer to move back to Santa Barbara that I didn't even question why there was a sudden desire to abandon New York. The move couldn't come at a better time, I was terrified of attending another year of school where another girl could point out that the medallions on my Tory Burch flats were slightly crooked.

Madison and me.

## Bad Boys, Bad Boys, Watcha' Gunna Do

My friend Madison lives in the biggest house I have ever seen. It's on top of a hill and you can see it from the Freeway. It looks like the palace of Versailles with marble floors, small, delicate furniture and parties every weekend. I spent most of my life at her house. Her mom, Ursula, was my mom's best friend. Every Friday night my mom and I would drive over to their house. My mom and Ursula would sit in the kitchen and talk about Ursula's ex-husband while Madison and I choreographed a dance to Lil John and the East Side Boyz' song 'Get Low'. At 10pm, my mom would wander into the basement to find us laying on the floor, tired from practicing our moves.

"Can I spend the night?" I would beg with a mouthful of Gushers.

"Sure." My mom would always say yes.

She would then pick me up on Sunday night and repeat this process all over again the next Friday. We usually had our sleepovers there because she had activities and junk food. My house on the other hand had talking-tos and carrot sticks. The one time Madison and I slept at my house my mom spotted us peeing in the yard "because we were bored".

In 2012, one year into ALS, my mom, David and myself found ourselves staying with Madison's family for about three months. I will always remember their house smelling of Ursula's hairspray, Frederic Fekkai, she was so fancy. We had decided to move in Paris before my senior year of homeschool high school was set to begin. When told about this plan I had a meltdown about the move as expected. But, right before we were about to go, David got a job in Los Angeles.

I'm not too sure what David's job is, but it has to do with electronics. He owns a company that essentially pimps out your hotel or home to a smart house, I think. Either that or he is the employee of the month at Radio Shack, he's very good with electronics.

We had already ended the lease at our house, we're renters not buyers. But, now without Paris in the future, we had no where to stay. The Nesbitts were kind enough to let us three stay at their house for as long as needed. We had already started to look for a new house, since we knew very well that we were not easy house guests. My mom came with an entourage of two nurses and five contraptions, while David really liked to make himself home wherever he went, this meant installing his own home theater 20 inches from the end of the bed.

One thing about David is that he loves TV. Not the actual shows, but physical televisions. His car had four TV's in it. Two for the backseat on the headrests, one at the center screen and one in the pull down mirror of the passenger seat. Since the invention of the Iphone, his driving has declined. He uses not one, but two phones to text while driving. One in each hand and a knee is used to steer. He had not crashed yet, but on the bright side, when he does, he'll get to enjoy an episode of Roseanne while waiting for the paramedics.

About two months into our stay at the Nesbitts, everyone was really feeling like this was our new home. Madison and I were both homeschooled at the time so we rarely left her bedroom. We didn't need to, there was a mini fridge outside her door just in case we didn't have the energy to walk to the kitchen. You'd be grossed out if you knew how many times this mini fridge was restocked.

Every night at 8pm, we would refuel in the kitchen. I had this theory at the time that if I binged before I slept, I would wake up skinnier. I wasn't wrong through, every morning after I pigged out, I would wake up with a noticeably flat stomach. So naturally I put that hypothesis together and thus my long elaborate food rituals were born. Since I wasn't eating much during the day because I was busy sleeping, I basically had one big meal when the sun went down. I knew this wasn't healthy, but I never looked better. I have tried this method recently and found out that my metabolism isn't what it used to be.

One particular night, Madison and I had just finished our three course meal in her kitchen and decided it was time to catch up on a nice episode of 'Husbands Who Kill' before going to bed. She headed to our "wing" of the house a few minutes before me, while I hung around the kitchen trying to decide what our after dinner, dinner would be. I landed on a bowl of instant oatmeal. It was the dinosaur egg kind. I nuked the oatmeal and walked the legitimate 5 minute long walk back to Madison's bedroom.

You know that feeling of being watched? A sense of being followed? Where you instinctively look behind you before the thought that someone is there even enters your mind. I felt this, did the normal quick glance behind my shoulder and saw something I never imagined could ever happen to me, a white girl in a nice neighborhood.

Behind me was a man, or a boy, he was clearly in 20's. He had on a black ski mask, had a black backpack and also a gun. He had it pointed at me as I walked towards the bedroom door. He didn't yell anything at me, no typical "This is a robbery," speech that I had so many times in movies before.

He just kept walking towards me with the gun, making me going into autopilot and also just keep walking. I was only a few steps away from Madison's bedroom at that point so once I hit the door, she saw what was happening too. We both first thought it was her brother playing a mean joke on us with a bb gun. He hadn't done anything like that before, or ever actually left his room, but I think our minds just had a first reaction of "There's no fucking way this is happening."

"Is this a joke?" Madison asked standing near the bed.

"This isn't a FUCKING JOKE. This is a FUCKING ROBBERY. Where is the FUCKING GOLD?" He shouted at us, overcompensating for his fear by swearing more than necessary. He already got his fucking point across.

The fear hit my body like lightning. I dropped my oatmeal. I knew this was real but somehow I couldn't accept it. I kept asking, "Cody what are you doing?" My cousin Cody was Madison's brother, Ashton's best friend. He might pull a prank like this, I thought. Right? I hoped he would.

"Who's Cody? Is he here?" The robber demanded. I'll refer to the robber as just the robber. It sounds old timey. And he was giving off an old timely vibe, because of the fact he asked where the gold was. Was he picturing gold bars stacked while Mr. Nesbitt sat upon them smoking a cigar and yelling at a maid to draw him a bath?

The robber made us lay halfway on the bed, our feet still touching the ground, so he could tie us up. When our faces were pushed against the bed, and we couldn't see the robber, I felt the gun against the back of my head. This is where I thought it was all over. He was going to shoot us in the head and rob the house. I don't know where the gun went while he zip tied our hands together, but there was no way Madison nor I were going to try to pull something. Watching all those crime shows over the years, I thought I would be prepared for a situation like this. I pictured this was the moment my adrenaline would kick in and I would roundhouse kick the guy in the face, grabbing his gun mid air and shooting him, execution style. This was merely a fantasy though. I could not move, I could not talk.

"Is anyone else here?" He shouted at us.

"No it's just us." Madison said, she knew I wasn't going to say anything. My voice box had packed up it's suitcase and walked out of this situation. I wish I could have gone with it. It wasn't just us at the house either. Ashton was in the bedroom next door. You would have thought he would have heard the commotion but he was busy playing World of Warcraft. Also, my mom and David were on the other side of the house in the "guest wing".

"Where's the safe?" He asked.

"I don't know." Madison quickly replied

"Where is it?" He asked again.

This is where Madison probably saved our lives, she calmly said, "I'll take you to it." I was instructed to "not fucking move," while they went to open the safe. Thank god he added the extra "fucking" into that sentence or else I wouldn't have known not to move.

At this moment, I was alone in the bedroom and I heard them walking away. I saw my phone on the bedside table, and being an amateur gymnist, I was able to grab the phone with my hands behind my back, unlock the iPhone and call my most recent number, David. I should have called 911 and I don't know why I didn't. I didn't have time to even think at this moment. By the time I had gotten David on the phone, I heard the robber in the background of the other line. Madison had taken him to my mom and David. I panicked and hung up the phone and hid it under the pillow.

I didn't even have time to imagine what was happening in the other room, because before I knew it, he was back. I was now alone with him.

"Alright I'm taking you over to the others." He said as he scooped me up and threw me other his shoulder like a salami. Like one of those big salamis in Europe that people carry over their shoulder.

My mind went into hyper-mode. I had seen Taken many times. Before I went to Italy with my school, my only requirement was to watch Taken and then report on what I would have done differently to avoid that situation. This was not homework given to me by my school, but given to me by my mom.

He had started walking towards the other end of the house, a good five minute walk. I started calling out in my head everything I saw, in case I needed to be the key witness later on. Nike backpack, size 9 feet, 5'10", brown hair, flat ass. I made a checklist in my mind and stored it for later, sincerely hoping there was a later.

I can't even imagine what the robber thought when he walked into my mom and David's room. My mom was laying on the bed with her personal and portable sleep number mattress, a breathing mask on her face that slightly resembles Jason from Friday the 13th and David was wearing a towel. Well, two towels, one around his waist and one had his hair wrapped up in like a girls spa day.

When he placed me on the ground between Madison and David, I started to calm down and rationalize with myself. He wasn't going to kill us, he would have already done that. If nothing goes wrong with his plan, he had no reason to kill us. I saw my mom's face and it was different than mine, she wasn't panicked or crying, she had a glare in her eye as if someone had eaten her first born in front of her.

He noticed the table of phones that David had set up in her homemade charging station. There were a minimum of five phones on that table. The robber unplugged all of them and tossed them out of the window in the garden.

I remember him referring to Madison's dad by his name, Pat Nesbitt. "Where is Pat Nesbitt." I thought it might have been a hit with a side of robbery. Pat was rich and powerful and probably had at least twelve people who wanted him dead. How else would he know his name.

"He's out to dinner, he's at Lucky's, he'll be home soon." My mom said so slowly and calmly. She kept turning to me and Madison on the floor and telling us she loved us. We were crying and mouthing it back to her. David was next to me, still in a towel and did the thing he always does in a time of panic, he kisses your forehead. He would later do this to me again when I was getting lip injections. So there we were, just waiting there with our dicks in our hand, waiting for Pat and Ursula to come home from their dinner, also secretly hoping they were bringing leftovers.

"Do not hurt them." My mom repeated to him, "Do not hurt them. Do not remove my breathing mask, do not touch it. I cannot move, I'm paralyzed."

Bet he wasn't expecting that. He started to pace around the room. The room was quite large, probably the biggest bedroom he had ever been in, so he might have just been counting steps to get the square footage for his story he would tell his friends.

"Are you ok? You look nervous" My mom asked him. This is where she lost me, was she making small talk with our captor? I don't know Stockholm syndrome could kick in this fast.

"This is my first time doing this." He replied. Uhhhhh

"Take a seat and breathe." My mom instructed him. "You just need to stay calm. But, can you help me with something. I'm a little cold. Can you put the blanket from the chair onto me."

The robber obliged. He took the Hermes cashmere throw and gently draped it over her legs, tucking her in. Us three on the floor were dumbfounded. Were they going to keep up with the Kardashian's next?

He walked across the room and took a seat on the itsy bitsy chair. He kept the gun pointed at us and asked, "This wind is crazy isn't it?" It was now the portion in the evening that small talk was necessary.

"Yeah, I hope there's not a fire." My mom replied.

"I was here last year for the big one, a buddy of mine lost his house in it." The robber continued, "The air after the fire is always the worst part." I kept mental notes of the information about himself that he was practically handing me.

After some idle gossip, we saw the Nesbitt's car pull up in the driveway. Everything was about to change. Dare I say, we were comfortable at this point in the robbery?

"Nobody move a fucking muscle." The robber said to us quietly as he made his way towards the bedroom door. He was also back to his big boy voice.

The four of us waited patiently as we heard Ursula screaming as he met her and Pat at the front door. He quickly walked them back into what was now the hostage room with their hands already tied. He pushed them onto the ground and tied up their ankles. Ursula was doing a hell of a lot of talking for someone who was new in town. There was something about hearing them see the robber for the first time that made my fear jump back up to 100. I was in their shoes just moments before, they were completely oblivious to the danger that lay ahead.

"Ok, how do I get to the safe?" He asked Pat as soon as they were bound up on the floor.

"You're going to go down the hall, to left, all the way down that hall, to the left again and up the stairs, take the second left and then a quick right. It's in that closet." Pat instructed him to do.

"And what's the code."

"18-22-09" Pat said without hesitation.

Then the robber left, we were alone and there were six of us. How was he able to overpower all of us? We were smarter than him and he wasn't even that big. But, he had a gun and that was enough to stop us from even thinking of something funny. Except Ursula, she must have thought that she was stronger than a gun. She had managed to wiggle out of her hand ties and was about to head over to the panic button right outside the room. Bad idea. We all whisper yelled at her to get back down on the ground. This was the only time I ever raised my voice at Ursula. She was about to get us killed if she couldn't get her wrist back into the restraints.

"Shit, where is it again?" The robber had walked back in, shaking his head at the fact that he got lost on the way to the safe.

Pat explained the same directions to him and he went off once more on his quest for tax free wealth. The house is extremely confusing with lots of twists and turns. Lots of distractions too, there's a candy bowl in the living room that always derails me. He got lost two more times, before the robber accepted Pat's offer to lead him to it.

"Ok, but don't try anything mister." It seems the robber had gotten the vast majority of his robbing vocab from a Cartoon Network bank robbery episode. The robber and Pat left the room, again leaving us alone. For a hostage situation, we were left unsupervised for a big chunk of it.

After about ten minutes, we started to get worried. We hadn't heard any gunshots or any loud noises, but room where the safe was held was practically in a different timezone, we wouldn't be able to hear anything anyways. This weird moment of waiting for the robber to come back for us felt like a lifetime.

Was this really happening? I didn't think anything worse could happen to us. It was just one blow after the next ever since ALS came into the picture. It was like I was living that inevitable plane crash episode of every show ever. "Oh we crashed!" "And we crashed on a cannibal island" "And now there's an earthquake!" I had assumed that God figured ALS was enough shit for one person and by the law of association, I was off the hook for any other bad things for at least ten years. Or maybe, we weren't to dissimilar to the Kennedy's and we also had a curse. That would be a welcomed plus at this point.

Finally, Pat and the robber stepped back into the room. The robber waved his little backpack around, letting us hear the jewelry clanking against each other. It was very loud, maybe there were gold bars in that safe.

"Listen to all that." He bragged to my mom. He was now officially confused by the friendship he had formed with my mom. "Ok, I'm leaving now. Nobody fucking move."

He backed out of the room and took the side door from the guest bedroom into the driveway. A smart move to avoid getting lost again and really embarrassing himself. And just like that, he was gone. We contemplated moving right away, but everyone just stayed put for a few minutes. Ursula had wiggled out of her restraints again and was instructed to go to the first aid kit in David's suitcase and grab the scissors.

David loved a first aid kit and considered it a travel must have. Anything to do with health, he is all about. For my birthday one year, he gave me a personal bathroom pharmacy, the works.

Ursula found the scissors and began uncutting the zip ties one by one. Our wrists were red from almost two hours of pressure against them. The panic button was hit as we barricaded ourselves into that room. Madison and I were instructed to hide in the bathroom, lock the door and call 911, because of course there was a landline in the bathroom. I love talking on the phone in the bath, I'm not being sarcastic.

That was the only 911 call I have ever made and I hope to never make another one. When you have to say out loud what you just experienced, that's when it all hits. I started crying while trying to get help, crying from fear, from relief and just disbelief. We got lucky. No one was hurt, no one was shot and it was over.

Not more than five minutes later, the entire army was there. The Nesbitt's clearly had the platinum membership in whatever panic button company was still around. I didn't know a panic button was a real thing outside a bank. This year for Christmas, I would like one for my home. But this was also their only line of defence for their massive property. The only security they had was clean up not prevention. From the outside, the house looked like a fortress, with stone walls and iron gates. But, as soon as you rang the call box at the gate, you were let in, usually no questions asked.

"Who is it?" The Nesbitt's housekeeper was tasked with answering the gate calls.

"Osama bin Laden"

"OK"

And just like that, you were in and welcomed with a cocktail at the door.

We were all dusted for fingerprints and Madison and I had to walk them through exactly what happened since we had the first interaction with him. Crime scene photos were taken of our wrists and the zip ties. Then, with their minimal security system, they caught an image of the robber on the security camera. He was walking towards the basement door and looked dead into the camera and just walked right in. There was no struggle, he just let himself in. From the basement, he entered the gym and from there, up the stairs and into the hallway. This is where he ran into me. I always think that if I hadn't needed some microwavable oatmeal, then I would have already been in the bedroom and not being followed. Or if I had taken a little more time in the kitchen, I would have seen him first and had a few extra seconds to figure out what to do.

But, it happened the way it happened and I'm thankful for that. I'm not thankful for the actual robbery, it didn't teach me any valuable lessons other than to always be packing heat. It made me angry and scared. I lost some of my innocence that night. I was only seventeen years old when this happened. I should have been much older to have my first traumatic event. If this had happened when I was fifty, then I would only have to relive it in my mind for another forty years or so. But, it happened when I was 17, that means I have to continue to look over my shoulder for the rest of my life. I'm only thankful that it ended how it ended with the gun never going off. I don't think I could handle having a facial scar.

They never caught the guy. They were able to figure out that he was young, but no duh. No old guy has the balls to take six people hostage like that. That was just stupid, but I guess it paid off. Literally. They discovered that the guy had a car parked at the end of the driveway, on the other side of the gate. He jumped the gate and was in the property. This jump is easy, it's something I did many times when I forgot their gate code. I would jump from the stone wall, over the gate, walk pass the sensor, and the gate would open. They never found any of the jewelry that he had stolen. The diamonds and gemstones he took were so huge that it was easy to break them up and sell everything separately I always thought. As for the gold bars, I'm not sure what he did with those.

If the authorities ever did catch this guy, I would start a Go Fund Me campaign to end his life. The Go Fund Me would raise enough money to purchase myself an AK47. Then, after harboring support at the polls and from the county officials, I would be allowed to shoot him in the face. I have never wanted to shoot anyone so badly. The closest to me being this angry at one single person was the girl at CVS the other day who gave me a snooty attitude when my debit card was declined. Then I would do a victory lap around his body and yell at the moon, "THIS IS REVENGE!!"

## Whippets and Kidney Stones

I was born at Cottage Hospital in Santa Barbara, CA on August 10th, 1995. I had been to the hospital twenty times after that. When I was three years old, my cousin Aidan and I were jumping on the bed and fell off. I don't have any memory of this, but from my mom's dramatized rendition, this is what happened. Aidan and I were upstairs, left alone to watch TV. It was rare for me to be left alone, I had to sit inside the grocery cart until I turned 12. After a few minutes, everyone downstairs heard a huge "thump" coming from the ceiling above. Someone rushed upstairs and found both of us on the floor. Because I am an O'Connell, everything is an emergency. The ambulance came and diagnosed Aidan with a concussion and me with a "bump on the head". It was advised that we be watched closely for any signs of brain damage. I like to think that this "bump on the head" is why I can't spell.

Once the paramedics left, my mom immediately rushed me to the hospital, only to be told that I was fine. I have been rushed to the hospital about fifteen times, every time resulting in glares from the nurses and phrases like, "We have real emergencies to tend to, ma'am." I went to the hospital once for a cold. I'm as embarrassed as you are.

I've been in trouble the same amount of times I've been seriously injured. Never. I never did anything that warranted real punishment in high school. I didn't have enough friends to get in trouble. I also was homeschooled, so the ability to make bad choices wasn't really an option for me. Even if I went out looking for trouble, the worst I could do would be to end up in chat room for roleplaying Hannah Montana. Homeschooling breeds losers, like me.

I had been homeschooled on and off my entire high school life. I started out ninth grade taking online courses. I took two weeks in October to try out public school. It didn't go very well, mainly because I didn't know the proper way to start a conversation. These were New York City teenagers, they didn't watch Disney Channel like I did. We had nothing in common. So, I walked out of school one day and never came back. I finished ninth grade from home. When tenth grade rolled up, homeschooling was the obvious choice. But, by October, I got the itch again. I enrolled in a private all-girls high school to finish the year. At the end of that school year, my mom was diagnosed with ALS and we were moving back to Santa Barbara. I didn't want to go to the public school in Santa Barbara because it had a daycare for the student's babies. Yes, the student's babies. Homeschooling it was then. I prefer homeschooling too, no one can call you out for wearing the same pants four days in a row through the computer.

In my junior year I finally started hanging out with people in real life and canceled my Club Penguin subscription. My friend from middle school, Masie, and I reconnected over our love of trying to become groupies. We attended every single concert we could afford. We would buy tickets to see bands based solely on the drummer's haircut. The venue we attended regularly in Santa Barbara was divided into two sections, over 21 and babies. I didn't have a fake I.D. because I was going through an involuntary straight edge phase.

The thing I loved about concerts wasn't actually the music. I love getting dressed up for something. My getting ready process takes about two full days. I begin by browsing the Nordstrom sale rack and purchasing anything my part-time babysitter salary would allow me. It usually was a t-shirt that didn't fit. It didn't matter, it was new, so I would wear it. Then, I would start applying Jergens self tanning lotion in three hour intervals, to speed up the process. It usually just left me smelling like bread and slipping on leather furniture. The day of whatever local band was playing, I would go to Sephora and get samples. I couldn't afford to buy real makeup but I already thought I was too good for L'Oreal. It never even crossed my mind to steal the makeup. I would see girls pocketing a Nars 'Orgasm' blush and get away with it all the time. I didn't have a problem with the morality of stealing, I had a problem with getting in trouble.

I was raised to believe that if I ever did something wrong, my throat would be slashed. So, I would gather up all my hard earned samples, copy a tutorial from Allure and call it a day. The actual concert portion of the evening was always a letdown. We never met the bands and ran away with them on tour. We never were spotted in the crowd and pulled on stage a la Courtney Cox. We would just bob our heads along with the music and go home only have talked to each other.

My mom was diagnosed with ALS one year before and the only person that knew was Masie. I was already ostracized for being homeschooled, I didn't want to be treated like a bigger outcast if everyone knew that I had to feed my own mom. So, it was just Masie and me for a while. Masie would come over and we would watch reality TV with my mom in bed and make noodles with butter. We were happy not having a social life, until we weren't.

This was in 2011, so Facebook was still the major form of

communication. We would scroll for hours watching everyone around us go out to parties and talk to boys, and most importantly, have somewhere to wear their cute outfits to. We wanted in. Masie did all the heavy lifting. She had already graduated from high school, and she wasn't homeschooled. She had the balls to get in contact with people who would actually know of parties in town. So, by next weekend, we found a college party to go to.

I wasn't allowed to do anything in high school. There was no trust in me that I would make good decisions, even though I had never made a bad one. My mom believed that I never did anything bad only because I wasn't allowed out of the house. She didn't have any faith in me making smart choices. She once read my texts and grounded me for texting someone "I think I should dye my hair black." Looking back, I'm happy that I didn't dye my hair black, but it should have been my choice. I grew angrier and angrier every time I was denied permission to do something. But, I didn't have the courage to not ask for permission, it didn't even cross my mind! That was something rebel teenagers did in Friday Night Lights, that wasn't real! I was so closed off from the real world, I didn't know that I was supposed to sneak out of the house or flirt with boys or try coffee. I thought everyone was living like they were an inmate.

I started to consider the idea that I should just go to this party, I shouldn't even ask. "No that's not a good idea." I caught myself saying out loud alone. "You can't do that."

After angrily pacing my room and trying on outfits I would wear to the college party, I finally decided to just ask if I could go. I had never been to a party that didn't have parental supervision before, it was time I tried beer. No, I wouldn't try beer, but I would hold a cup of it all night and pretend!

"Hi Mommy." I still called my mom Mommy and I was seventeen years old. I stood at the door frame of her bedroom, for the first time nervous to go in.

My mom was lying in her bed, propped up with Tempurpedic triangles and pillows under every limb. I had never asked her to go to a party before, I didn't know how this usually went down. I thought the most casual thing would be to sit on the side of her bed and talk about what I was going to have for lunch.

Once it was decided that I was going to make pancakes for lunch, it was time to ask the question.

"Do you want to make tacos for dinner?" She asked me, knowing the answer would obviously be yes.

But, at the same time she asked her question, I asked mine. "Can I go to a party tonight?"

"Sure, who's party?" She assumed it was a small Montecito dinner party where I would network and exchange SAT scores.

"Masie's friend."

"Do I know them?"

"No, they went to Laguna." Laguna was the private school in Santa Barbara and my mom trusted all private school kids because she was dumb when it came to things like that. Private schools breed date rapists with bad expensive haircuts. Just look at Brett Kavanaugh.

"Will their parents be home." That was the question I knew she would ask. Of course, the parents wouldn't be home. Why would someone's parents be hanging out at UCSB in a house where the couches were in the front yard.

"Yeah." And just like that, I lied.

But, because I had spent many hours watching Gossip Girl, I knew my way around a con. My plan was to get permission to go to a fake party that was up to my mom's standards, show her how excited I was to go, let her help me choose my outfit, and promise to be home by eleven. Then, a few hours before this supposed party was to begin, tell her it was canceled, act devastated and then get the text from Masie that I would read out loud to my mom.

"Oh!" I perked up from laying on her bed. "The party was moved! Masie just texted me that the parents had to cancel Annabella's (fake person) birthday party because the house had a leak but her brother is going to host it at his house. I gotta go get dressed!"

"Woah, woah, wait. Who's her brother, where does her brother live?" She began to ask.

"Let me find out. I heard he has a really nice place on the beach." I wasn't lying, his frat house was technically on the beach, all of frat row was on the beach. This was Santa Barbara.

After an hour of back and forth and supplying somewhat true information, it was agreed that I could go. I just had to be back by eleven.

The eleven curfew was going to be a problem. I wasn't allowed to drive in other people's cars without a helmet, so I was going to pick up Masie and a few other people and drive everyone there. The party was 20 minutes from my house, and after all the carpool stops, it would take me 40 minutes to actually get to the party. Then, to return, it would take another 40 minutes. The party didn't start until 10 pm and we couldn't show up until 10:30 because it would be social suicide if we arrived on time. I would have to turn around as soon as I got there in order to make curfew. I was basically an Uber before Uber was invented. This was going to be a Mission Impossible. I had to get my curfew extended.

"Please, I won't even be able to go if I have to be home by eleven. I never go anywhere, please, just this one time, can I be home by 12. Please?" I begged and got into prayer position. This was a long shot, I had never even been awake at 12 let alone outside the house. I didn't think I would even want to be out at that hour, I was so exhausted from all this bargaining. I said a silent prayer to the party gods and waited for an answer,

"Ok, but if you are home even one minute after twelve, I'm going to take away your jeans."

My mom knew that being grounded didn't work for me because I loved staying in my room, but my jeans. Don't touch my jeans. "Ok, I promise. Thank you!" I wrapped my arms around her body. I immediately felt bad. Why did I even want to go out and hang with people I didn't even know. I should be home with my mom, I didn't have much time left with her. But, that feeling was gone the second I walked into my room to text Masie that the plan was on. I knew my priorities were out of whack.

Operation college party was underway, I had successfully picked up everyone from their parent's house and we were looking for a parking spot. I had taken David's Escalade so parking would be a bit of a bitch. It was 10:45 and I was trying to parallel park for the first time. I was under the impression that valet would be available. I gave up and parked on the sidewalk.

I entered the house wearing what I thought was Miley Cyrus chic. I had on Levi cut off shorts that are still in my closet to this day, a pair of cowboy boots that no cowboy would be caught dead in, and a turtleneck sweater. The look could only be described as "religious hooker." I had left the house earlier that night in jeans and changed in the car into shorts. I did not realize that this move would later take away 10 minutes I desperately needed to get home before curfew. My mom wouldn't let me wear the shorts out of the house but I thought my legs were my best asset. I learned that my butt is actually my best asset but I don't own any assless chaps.

The house was filled with ten times over the maximum occupancy limit and there were definitely no parents there. The air was filled with smoke and I worried that my cashmere sweater would need to be dry cleaned after this. I hate smokers that aren't me. My only experience with college parties was from what I saw in Animal House. I thought I was going to be pressured into drinking, I had already come up with what I was going to say if someone tried to pour a shot down my throat.

As Masie and I were lingering around the kitchen looking for the chip bowl, two guys that looked somehow both 12 and 40 came over to us. Their hair was bleached from the sun and glowed under the Bud Light neon sign, but their skin looked like it had been roasted over an open fire. One looked like Dog the Bounty Hunter and the other looked like his wife.

"Hey, you girls want a drink?" One of them asked raising a Kirkland brand vodka bottle over their head.

"No thanks, I'm in AA," I replied.

"That's cool." The other one said putting on his Oakley sunglasses, even though it was night. And we were inside.

"And my probation officer is outside," I said trying to evacuate the conversation. I didn't have the faintest idea of how probation worked but they clearly didn't either.

"Have you guys ever tried whippets?" Dog the Bounty Hunter asked. He reached over to the fridge and pulled out a bottle of whipped cream.

Masie and I left the conversation and headed to the backyard. Another 100 people were outside gathered around a half pipe that was lit by tiki torches. A fire hazard in my book. We found a seat on a log and tried to have a conversation over the DJ blasting different Pitbull remixes. I couldn't focus on what Masie was saying because I was too busy listening in to all the conversations around me.

"Are you pledging Kai Beta Omega?"

"Bethany is driving me crazy, she was so drunk during rush last week."

"Kappa Kappa Gamma has the best sluts."

Was this really what I dreamed of? I pulled a splinter out of my thigh and rethought my choices of wearing shorts and wanting to join a sorority. I had always dreamed of going to a huge state school, working my

84

way up the ranks at the top sorority house, become the vice president (president was too much charity work) and eventually graduate and get an internship in PR. I wanted what I thought was the right way to do college. I even considered going to this college, UCSB, where Kappa had the best sluts. It was September and I was in the process of sending out all my college applications. I had applied mainly to New York schools like NYU and The New School, a few state schools on the west coast and The University of Paris because I was forced to.

I checked my phone for the time. 11:10. I had to leave in 10 minutes. I didn't mind leaving, I felt ashy and sticky at the same time.

"Masie can you go find everyone? I'm going to bring the car around. I have to leave, like now." I said standing up.

We separated and began the mission of getting me home on time. The walk to my car would be sobering if I had taken a drink. The front patios of all the houses were illuminated by the fluorescent street lamps, giving everything a grey tone. I didn't want to spend another 10 minutes here, let alone 4 years. All these kids thought this was the center of the world, and that whipped cream whippets were real whippets. I began to imagine what my life would be like if I decided to go to this school or any other school like it. Even though I had blonde hair, I probably wouldn't get into the best house. I would maybe get into the third best house if I wore tighter clothes. I would never make friends because everyone here just wants to go to the beach, and I don't like to swim. I would spend every Saturday night walking up and down this street, hoping to stumble into a party, always being disappointed when I finally found one. And I would probably gain the Freshman 15 from all the beer alone.

Midway through my self evaluation, I reached the car. I drove back to the party where Masie was waiting with 2 of the 3 other people I was supposed to drive back.

"Where's Kelly?" I asked Masie as she was getting in.

"She said she wanted to stay, she found a different ride home," Masie said as I began to drive away.

The drive from UCSB to the freeway is about 10 minutes. As I was getting on the freeway at 11:30, Kelly called.

"Can you come pick me up, I can't find my ride anymore. I think he left." She said slightly slurring.

My mental math went into overdrive, I didn't have time to go back and get her and make it home before 12. My first thought was to leave her at the party since I usually play by an every man for themselves mentality, but I couldn't leave her to become another Dateline episode. So, I went back.

It was now 11:45 and I was 20 minutes from home. I was screwed. My mom kept calling but I didn't know how to disable Bluetooth and I couldn't let my mom hear Kelly crying in the backseat. She would know it was alcohol induced. My mom was never an oblivious parent, she always knew when I was bullshitting. She also never went to sleep before I came home like all the other parents do. I knew she would be waiting for me to come back, shotgun placed in her hand by her caregiver Paulina.

I had successfully dropped everyone off at Masie's house since there was no way I was doing multiple stops. I sped down my street and stopped the car in the church parking lot next to my house. I had to change back into pants. In a church parking lot. I should have made some calls here about what was more important, the pants or curfew.

I walked into the house at 12:15 wearing pants. I was grounded and jeanless by 12:16.

The next morning I woke up to David walking into my room. Knocking wasn't our thing.

"We have to go to the hospital." He said as I sat up.

"But I was only 15 minutes late!" I cried, thinking they were committing me.

"No you douchebag, for mom. You have to come with."

"What's wrong now?" I asked standing up and following him to their room. It was normal for my mom to cry hospital. With ALS, every little thing has to be treated like a life or death situation, because it was. If she was nauseous, we went to the hospital. With ALS, you can't throw up, you'll choke and die on your own vomit. If she felt light headed, we went to the hospital. It could be because her breathing machine wasn't functioning properly and she could die.

I became a hospital regular. I was familiar with the hospital because of my mom's overreacting when I was a kid, but now it was serious. She had been experiencing sharp pains in her stomach for the past few days but it had become too much to handle now.

We rolled up to Cottage Hospital with our entourage. Me, my mom, David, and Paulina. Paulina was my mom's favorite caregiver. David called her a caretaker because he didn't know the difference. She didn't treat my mom like she was sick and I think that's why she loved her so much. She also would arrive at our house in the morning, have a shot of tequila then share a cigarette with my mom and watch TV. She was perfect.

One good thing about ALS is that you don't have to wait in the waiting room at the ER, you just get to go in. It's also important to mouth "suckas" to the people with stab wounds sitting and reading an old Highlights magazine as you walk in. But, waiting in line is better than ALS, anything is better than ALS.

As we waited for the doctor, I kept glancing over at my mom. Her face remained stoic. She looked strong and brave, like this was no big deal. She didn't flinch when the nurse took three tries to get the I.V. in, she smiled at me instead. I wanted to reach out and hold her hand but I worried she would feel the fear I had running through my palms. Instead I read her the news from People Magazine.

The doctors began running tests on my mom while I sat and

watched with curiosity and disgust. There are two things I'm afraid of, needles and really long needles. This fear has gotten me out of ever having my blood taken and I've only had to have an IV once.

The only time I ever had to have an IV was when I got my wisdom teeth taken out. I'm not proud of how much of a baby I am when it comes to any type of medical produce. Especially after watching everything my mom had been through. Even before I have a shot, I have to mentally psych myself up. I tell myself that if my mom could handle ALS, I can handle a flu shot. I think about all the painful nerve conduction tests she had to endure and even her childbirth where she had to squeeze ten pound me out. But as soon as I'm 'roided out on this thought, I see the nurse come closer with a needle and we have to do the whole process over again.

Most people get their wisdom teeth out, its routine and over quickly, and most people do it while in high school. My overwhelming fear of having a needle anywhere near my arm or mouth, made it so I didn't go in for this procedure until 21 years old. If someone had told me that impacted wisdom teeth were going to make my bottom teeth crooked, I probably would have gone in sooner because I am vain.

I went in the day before my surgery for the preliminary visit and to ask any questions I might have.

"Are you going to put a needle in my arm and my mouth or just my arm? How long will I be out? Can I keep the teeth when I'm done? Where does the laughing gas come into play?"

The dentist looked at me like I was eleven and slowly explained the process to me, "I can give you laughing gas before any of this if you would like, but most patients are fine with just local anesthesia."

"I'm not most patients," I said crossing my arms so he knew I meant business.

"We can also prescribe anti-anxiety medication for before if you're nervous."

"Please do. Also, you didn't answer my other questions, where are the needles going?"

"If you are going to opt-in for general anesthesia, you won't be knocked out completely, you'll be awake but you won't remember anything. With this, first we'll put the anesthesia here," he pointed to my arm, "then we'll numb your mouth. You'll be done in a few hours but won't remember anything."

I pretended to be satisfied with his answer, but knew that I was stronger than medication and I would definitely remember the entire procedure. I took his Ativan prescription to fill and headed home, already shaking.

On the morning of the procedure, I woke up and took three pills and wished I had more. Once I sat down in the operating chair, I immediately began to cry. Crying is my first instinct in a lot of situations, it doesn't make me a good arguer or a good candidate for botox. The doctor strapped the laughing gas to my nose but I wasn't laughing. He then inserted the IV. Then, he was right, I don't remember anything. I love anesthesia. He was also right about me not being fully knocked out because I managed to take a photo of myself during the wisdom tooth extraction.

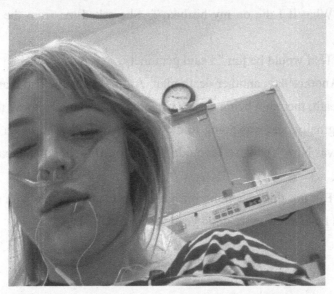

I didn't know that my minor procedure years later was nothing in comparison to what my mom was going through at the hospital. The doctor had informed her that she had kidney stones and she would have to be kept here until they passed. I knew a little bit about kidney stones because my science teacher once brought her own kidney stones to class in a mason jar to show us. They looked like fossilized lint balls.

Any time someone is in the hospital, they are exposed to more infections and diseases than they normally would be. In my mom's case, she was extra vulnerable to anything and made this very clear to the staff at Cottage Hospital.

"If I get a lung infection, I will sue every one of you until I die." She smiled sweetly to make the nurses believe she was joking, only so they wouldn't sue her. She was serious though.

Her stay was going well and she seemed happy to be on so many drugs. I was happy she was on so many drugs because she entirely forgot I was grounded. She was too busy enjoying the new wing of the hospital, complete with a Starbucks on each floor, a large TV that had both E! and Bravo and nurses that spoke English. The English was something that we soon learned to not take for granted.

"What if I die on my birthday?" She asked me from the hospital bed.

"That would be fun," I said genuinely.

Another day, another death plan. At this point she had many plans for her death, the main being assisted suicide so she could choose the exact date. Originally, she was going to die on Christmas, just to be an asshole. Then, it was New Years, so I wouldn't be inclined to go out and party very late.

"But not this upcoming birthday, don't suffocate me with a pillow just yet. I have a few more good years left in me."

*This photo of Laurie's apartment is OK because I've still*
*wearing my coat and you can't see my shoes.*

This photo at Chanel's apartment is OK because I'm still
wearing my coat and you can't see my shoes.

# Lessons I Learned From My Mom Only After Doing The Opposite

*Lesson 1: Dress classic, not trendy.*

I experienced one of the most special moments of my life and I can't share the pictures because I look like a vagabond. My mom scored us an invite to tour Coco Chanel's private apartment above the Chanel store on Rue Cambon.

"Make sure to wear that Chanel jacket and flats. Do not wear your lesbian boots!" My mom shouted to me over the phone before our visit.

Well, I didn't listen. I wore a black sweater with intentional distressing and my "lesbian boots." The sweater was Alexander Wang so I thought that would cancel out the distressing. As for the boots, there's no excuse. They were chunky, dirty and from Urban Outfitters. Everyone was wearing them, but that didn't make them right. I even wore a beanie. To Coco Chanel's apartment. I have the photos hidden in a file on my computer. Once I learn how to photoshop myself into an outfit that makes me look like a lady, not a crack whore, I'll share them.

*Lesson 2: Never eat while laying down, you'll choke.*

After a long day of class (3 hours), I picked up a ham and cheese sandwich from the boulangerie near my apartment. I never ate at my dining table alone because it was depressing, so I crawled into bed, turned on Modern Family and started to eat my dinner. The sandwich was as long as my arm, so I began to sink into bed while finishing it up. I was almost horizontal when I felt a piece of the tough bread stuck in my throat and unable to swallow. I sat up and kicked my laptop off the bed in a rush to get to some water.

I had to give myself the Heimlich over a chair before I could breathe again. After calming myself down, I went back to my computer, only to find the screen shattered and not usable. I didn't have my laptop for the rest of the semester nor did I eat laying down again.

*Lesson 3: You won't regret going somewhere, you'll regret staying home.*

I took the train to London over Easter weekend to see my friend Madison. The purpose of the trip was to go to an Easter Hunt at a royal's country house. It wasn't William or Harry, but they were distant relatives I believe. The night before, Madison and I went out to celebrate nothing and both ending up vomiting into the early hours of the morning. At noon the next day, I received a call from the car service that they were downstairs, ready to drive us to the estate.

"Do you want to just stay in and order room service instead?" Madison asked.

"Please!" I said over my hangover.

We never went to the Easter hunt and I never forgave myself.

*Lesson 4: Don't stray from your natural color, just enhance it.*

I was born a blonde and over the years my natural color turned into a mousey brown. I have very pale skin so a grey/brown color is not a good look on me, or anyone actually. In order to return to my toddler hair color, I would highlight my hair just enough to look like a brighter, better version of myself. Then, I decided to bleach my entire head platinum.

"It's not going to turn out like you think it will," My mom warned me.

I didn't listen. I left the salon with bright orange hair, a far cry from the photo of Miley Cyrus I used for inspiration. In an effort to cover up the damage, I went chocolate brown. I've been trying to get back to my original hair color ever since.

*Lesson 5: Wear sunscreen*

I am very pale, you can see my veins through my skin and sometimes even my organs. As a child, I was never let outside the house with SPF 60, but all I wanted was a natural sunkissed glow. When I went to Hawaii in 2011, I decided I was "too old" for sunscreen. My mom sprayed my body with sunscreen and I immediately jumped into the ocean in an effort to wash it off. How was I going to get a tan with all this on?

The next day, a red sunburn developed on back so deep that it blistered and I had to sleep on my stomach for the next week. I couldn't go to the beach for the rest of the trip. I even had to sit up straight on the plane ride, careful not to pop the blisters on the leather seat. I now wear sunscreen even on my hands.

*Lesson 6: Shyness turns to rudeness*

I have never been one to go up to someone and greet them. I didn't talk to any waiters for the first ten years of my life because I was too nervous to order. When I was 15, I went to a dinner party with my mom in New York. Because my mom is a networking queen, she convinced the fashion editor at Harper's Bazar to give me an internship. The next week I was alone on a photoshoot. My job was to go around and ask if anyone needed any assistance or a coffee. I was too shy to go up to anyone and help, so I just stood at the back of the room and waited for someone to tell me what to do. No one ever did, I didn't speak to anyone.

My mom had warned me that I would need to make an effort if I didn't want to come off as rude. I couldn't push past my fear of being perceived as annoying and desperate and instead came off as a rude, unhelpful little biotch. That was my first and last day of that internship.

## Blacklisted

David would have been a nurse in a previous life. Not a doctor though, because he doesn't wash his hands enough. But, a nurse because he loves to take care of people. After the first diagnosis of ALS, David took my mom to Paris to get an alternative opinion, clearly hoping for a different outcome. They came home empty-handed. They were only told what they had been told months before in stupid America. She had ALS and it wasn't going anywhere she wasn't going. ALS isn't the type of disease that you can turn off for a little bit and just deal with it later. It is visible at all times. From the polio legs to the swollen fingers, it is evident and there's no escaping it, not even for a second. Once ALS takes a limb from you, it's not coming back. There isn't a brief moment of movement ever again from the arm that stopped cooperating. Picture this if you really want to scare yourself. Freeze in the position that you are in now, I don't care if it's comfortable or not. Ok, need to move your arm slightly to the right? You can't. You have to call out for help to move even a centimeter to the right. Your body becomes claustrophobic of yourself. It's a trap and it's not going to give you a way out.

Did this all just become very negative? Well, that's ALS. There is no hope for a cure right now. Here's an idea though. Everyone loves money right? Create a prize for the doctor that figures out a cure for ALS. If they can come up with a cure, they can have the million dollars. I know it doesn't work that easily, but that's my hope.

I watched my mom try every single bat shit crazy treatment she was told about. That's how desperate she was to stay around. I know that I personally would have given up a lot sooner. I would not be able to go on thinking of anything but killing myself if I were given the same prognosis she was. But, that's because she was a better person than I ever will be. Except for that one time she said my cousin had Autism so we had to skip the line of Jekyll and Hyde's in New York City. That was when I was the better person for disapproving.

I've noticed with all the cases of ALS that I've heard of, the patient's first reaction is to search for another cause of the symptoms. One begins to hope for cancer! "Please let me have cancer." I've heard my mom say, "I'll even take MS." It's at this moment, you realize that ALS is the worst possible disease you could be told you have. I'm talking like I have ALS, I don't, I've barely ever had a cold. But, I saw first hand the ruin it can take on one's body.

There were a few surgeries that were recommended, but none that would be the cure all. We were told that my mom's breathing and eating would be the most important aspects to focus on and like no shit sherlock. I didn't know what a diaphragmatic pacer was at this point in my life. I probably shouldn't have become familiar with this device until me and everyone else around me started to get them when we were in our 70's. I also shouldn't have known what was an enema was, but here we were. I became well versed in medical jargon and can 100% keep up with Grey's

Anatomy even if I missed an episode.

The surgery for the pacer was going to hopefully prolong my mom's life by a year or so. We had begun to consider an extra year with my mom as a huge accomplishment since we were already two years in. But, this surgery could also cause some major complications. A surgery like this performed on someone in as fragile a state as my mom had upped the stakes by a good 50%. It had to work, because there was no other option. Hearing that death was a very possible outcome of the surgery, really made us all take a step back and weigh the options. But, in the end, it wasn't mine or David's or the doctor's or anyone else's choice but my mom's. She was not one to take risks, she didn't even cross the street without looking both ways. I was actually forced to hold her hand while crossing the street until we were the same height. But, she had weighed her options carefully. She could either take her chances or give up.

"We're going to make a small incision right at the rib cage, leaving the pacer to sit comfortably here." The doctor said, pointing to the right side of her chest.

"Will my boobs pop?" My mom was asking the hard hitting questions now. "I have implants, will they pop?"

"No." The doctor wasn't enjoying her questions.

After the consultation and the decision that my mom was a candidate for this risky procedure, we went to Jerry's Deli for some Matzah Ball Soup. The surgery was set to take place the following week and should take about two hours, but the recovery would take a month. I had assumed the word pacer, meant that it would pace itself. The piece would be installed, and the work would be done, the machine would carry on to pace my mom's lungs and breathing. In reality, the pacer would be a series of wires coming out right under my mom's boob. These wires would then be plugged into another machine, to zap her lungs into behaving. Ouch. But, my mom was at the point that this seemed like a pinch compared to what she had already endured just in ALS testing alone.

This was one of the first big surgeries in our family that wasn't elective. My mom and her entourage arrived at Cedars around 4 am. It was quite the Motley Crue. There was me, David, my grandmother, my aunt Bobbie-Anne, my cousin Julie, my dad Dylan and my aunt Heather. And this was just the 4 am shift.

It's very clear that David does not enjoy the company of my family, and with good reason. The last time he and Julie spoke was during a series of heated arguments back in 2006. The first argument was because she accidentally used his electric tea kettle on the stove and didn't replace it. The second was because she gave him a self-help book for his birthday. Here's the thing about Julie, she's hilarious and also insane. I went to go stay with her a few years ago at her house in Orcas Island. It's a very secluded island filled with Christmas trees and I think Twilight was shot there. She had broken up with her boyfriend a few months prior to my visit and the same night I landed she had become convinced that he was Black Ops and was going to come and kill her. She stood guard at the front door all day with a cocked shotgun just waiting. She even made me take the night shift.

"Wait, where's my iPod?" My mom asked after she had been stripped of everything but her tampon.

David came to her rescue and turned on her little iPod shuffle to her "surgery mix." I don't know if it can be called a mix because it was just Queen's "Under Pressure" and that big Hawaiian guy's cover of "Somewhere Over the Rainbow" on repeat. Then, they rolled her off through the doors and the fifteen of us stood there and waved. This might have been the only time my mom had an actual support system all together.

This was the first time I had ever been in the waiting room for someone to come out of surgery. It wasn't until the moment they rolled my mom away that I realized there was a very real possibility she might not come back. I have a habit of not understanding the severity of a situation or overreacting completely.

This could be it. She might not be rolled back out. What were my last words to her? "See ya." Oh, that's not how I wanted this to end. I began to pace around the waiting room and noticed the sun rising and illuminating the courtyard below us. I started to appreciate life and the beauty that I normally did not care for. A few minutes ago, my biggest concern was if I'll get to go to Taco Bell for lunch. I usually was allowed to get fast food in troubled times only. A tendency I still seem to hang on to.

My cousin Julie is my mom's cousin, so she's actually my second cousin. But, I've always called her Uncle Julie because of her strapping shoulders. She is the one who can make me laugh when I really am trying not to.

She leaned over and whispered to me, "I'm so excited to be your new mom." And everything was ok again.

"Do you want to go to the Cafeteria?" She asked.

Now, there's something you should know about me. My favorite meal is anything served cafeteria style. There are endless possibilities once I get that plastic tray in front of me. I usually go for a combination of chicken tenders and whatever Italian option is on the menu. Also, the mousse. Cafeterias always have chocolate mousse. We loaded up our trays with an inappropriate amount of lunch options considering it was 8 am and ate together in silence. Silence not only because there wasn't room in our mouths for words, but also a moment of silence for what was to come.

"Eleanor O'Connell's family?" A doctor asked looking in our direction

"Yes," David said, bracing himself for the news. The surgery had gone over the expected amount of time by almost two hours, so concerns were growing.

"She's in recovery, the surgery is complete and you can see her shortly." He said, as if she just had her tonsils removed and left.

We all took a sigh of relief and settled back into our chairs. David followed the doctor looking for more answers. He reported back that we could go see her once they transfer her over to intensive care.

"Why intensive care? Shouldn't she just be in recovery?" The group asked.

What the doctor had not told us at that moment, was that while the surgery was successful, there were some complications. One of her lungs had collapsed during the procedure. Could her luck get any worse? This was supposed to be a borderline routine operation with the chances of that happening being slim to none, but then again, chances of getting ALS in the first place are slim to done.

The group wobbled over the intensive care wing of the hospital, we looked like a pack of hyenas moving all together throughout the different wards. Intensive care is very exclusive, it has its own separate wing, with two glass corridors leading to and from the private rooms, with nurses stationed at each door. It was harder to get in there than Delilah's on a Friday. I would know, I've never been let in. There were strict rules too, you must be eighteen to enter and only two guests at a time per patient. David was obviously the first one to go in and say hello. I stayed back and argued with the guard that I just look really young for my age and I left my I.D. back in my Buick. He wasn't budging. I don't know if he was mad at me for being so persistent or just mad at the fact that he was a male nurse, but either way, he wasn't going to let me in.

"It's my mom. She's in a coma from her hysterectomy!" I yelled, hoping the use of the term hysterectomy would make him uncomfortable. "Please, she has chlamydia and might not make it much longer." It was like I was completely oblivious that he had her chart right in front of him.

"No I.D., no entrance." He said taking into account that I was wearing Uggs, as if no one over the age of eighteen wore Uggs. But, he would be wrong, David was wearing his Uggs that day too.

"Oh, hey, look I found it." I handed him my learner's permit, hoping the confidence would trick not only his morals but maybe his eyes too.

"This says your 16. You must be 18 to enter." He said handing back the card to me, not impressed.

"You're really not going to let her in? It's her mother, she'll be supervised by me and I'm over eighteen." My dad said trying to ease the situation.

"Nope, she'll just have to wait until the patient gets transferred to recovery. Rules are rules." He said, going back to his People Magazine, signaling the conversation was now over.

My dad and I backed away to hatch a plan to overpower this man who clearly had let the power go to his head. I had already shared too much information to go back in and tell the truth now. We left what was clearly this man's territory and went downstairs for a Starbucks, some fuel was needed if anything was going to get accomplished.

"I have a baseball cap and sunglasses in the car," I suggested. Maybe a disguise would work.

"No, they know you now. We can just wait 'til they switch shifts before trying again." My dad offered.

The fact that this hospital was not letting me see my mother, who was lying in for all they know, a coma, was insane to me. The over 18 rule was equally absurd. Did anyone under 18 carry a higher risk of spreading something to the vulnerable patients? I know it was obvious that I didn't wash my hair that frequently, but I didn't have Hep B or anything. I just wanted to say what's up to my mom.

After my second iced caramel macchiato and two bathroom breaks, I was ready for my very own break in. My dad and I had hatched a plan to get me into the ICU by using one of the glass walkways that lead to the opposite end of where we initially had tried. This passageway was typically used by doctors wheeling their patients to surgery so they didn't have to go through the waiting room. But today, it would also be used by me.

We wandered down to the courtyard to get a view of the glass passageway that I would have to infiltrate. This was my very own Zero Dark Thirty and I needed to come to terms with the fact that I could be kicked out of the hospital, or worse, the cafeteria. We watched the doctors pass through this walkway, all dressed in lab coats and all equipped with scanning badges. I had neither, but I was wearing a beige cardigan and that was pretty close right?

"You go man the other side of the door and let me in," I told my dad.

My dad and I made our split and hoped we'd see each other again on the other side. I had full faith in our plan to get me into the ICU and I didn't want to show up empty handed. After a quick stop in the gift shop for magazines and a card that had a cartoon teddy bear saying "You made it another year," I took the elevator up to the correct floor. Once I arrived at the doors that would lead to the glass corridor, I realized that this was going to be much easier than I thought.

In my mind, I was envisioning an obstacle course, full of rolling gurneys, maybe some amputated limbs and a vending machine just to test me. Nope, it was just an empty hallway that I had to cross aside from the few doctors making their way through. My small mind decided that if I had a limp, I could be mistaken for a patient, and no one would pay me any attention. I went searching for a face mask, unaware that those were generally reserved for the doctors and not the patients. I put on my mask, tied my neckerchief around my forehead and limped through the hallway. Yes, I was in my neckerchief phase at this time. It was a Gucci one and it was adorable.

About halfway through the one minute walk, so 30 seconds into the mission, I was approached by a nurse passing by.

"Excuse me, are you lost?" She asked, assuming I had gotten on the wrong bus after my teen special needs day out, ended up here and somehow sprained my ankle in the process.

"Are you?" I asked back. I found that answering a question with a question is best when you don't have an answer. Since I only had 15 more steps until I was in the clear, I kept moving. Never looking back.

The American Sign Language that I had taught myself kicked in once I was nearing the exit, signing for my dad to open the door. I had mastered only the alphabet at this point in my lessons. I thought that if I knew the alphabet, I could sign any word I wanted. I thought highly of myself for being the first one to discover this shortcut. My next lesson, I learned that the language did not work this way. He didn't understand but got the idea and opened the door for me.

"You look like Rambo," He said to me as I entered the ICU.

"You don't know what I've been through," I replied dramatically and followed his lead to my mom's room.

Entering her room was the first time I saw her truly sick and also in a full face. Yolanda was in the room with my mom and was in the middle of completing my mom's smokey eye when I entered. There was no way my mom would die without some lip liner.

My mom had been sick for about a year, but this was the first time it seriously showed. Her hospital gown, while never flattering, hung off her like a potato sack without potatoes. She had finally hit her goal weight of 100 pounds. Her hair was damp with sweat, the winged eyeliner was dripping off, and she didn't have the energy or the strength to lift her head at this point.

I closed the door behind me, remembering that I was still "on the run." I walked over to my mom and sat at the edge of the bed. Now, I'm not a very nurturing person. I don't really know what to do in a situation like this or any situation actually. It's best if I'm left out. I tried to hold my mom's hand but was woken out of my silence when I squeezed her hand and she couldn't squeeze back.

"Are you ok?" I asked already knowing the answer, "What happened?"

She looked at me with sunken eyes, "Mom's been raped." She said referring to herself before bursting out laughing.

She did look like she had just been raped, which also made us laugh because we are both wildly inappropriate. We let out a sigh of relief and I tried to brush down her "sex hair".

"Do you wanna watch anything?" She asked, knowing I would want to.

I turned on Sex and the City, something I could always count on being on some channel at all times.

I used to not be allowed to watch this show and if you've ever seen it, you would know why. But, because my mother didn't want me to grow up and not know this major culturally relevant piece of history, she caved and let me watch. But, I had to watch it with her. I was about 7 when I started watching this show and I loved it. I didn't know what was happening in it most of the time but it made me sure that I wanted to be thirty, sexy and rich. Sadly, none of this has happened yet.

I didn't ask what sex was until I was watching the news over breakfast one morning when I was in the 5th grade. There was a news story about someone being a test tube baby.

"What's a test tube baby?" I asked, opening up a can of worms that would be directly sprinkled over my Frosted Flakes.

My mom's approach to the "talk" wasn't so much about how when a man and a woman love each other very much and want to express that love. I think this wasn't her approach because it wasn't something she was familiar with. Like I said, I think I was the product of a one night stand, or at the very least, a friends with benefits situation gone wrong. She went the scientific route. I learned the word ovary that day and left for school even more confused than I had usually been.

Sitting in her hospital room, I was immediately taken back to when I used to snuggle up in her bed and watch Sex and City with my mom. If there were a pair of heels in the room I would have gladly put them on, for a more interactive viewing experience. This little fantasy bubble burst when a nurse came into the room.

"Uhm, excuse me, ma'am." She said directly referring to me as ma'am.

"Yes, sir?" I retorted back with a statement that both answered her initial question and told her to get an upper lip wax all at once.

Clearly not amused with me, she looked at me with eyes that were typically reserved for teachers before they told me to stop distracting my peers.

"You're not allowed in here." She said pointing at me.

"Who me?" I asked looking around the room as if there was someone else behind me.

"Yes, you." She said, "We saw you sneak in here."

"What do you mean sneak in, she's my daughter." My mom came to my defense.

"Yes, but guests of any relationship are not allowed in here if they are under 18. Visiting hours will resume once you check out." The nurse was clearly not a fan of this entire room nor my entire family.

"I am 18 though. I don't know what you're talking about. I think you have the wrong number ma'am." I replied before turning back to the television.

"We have it on our surveillance camera your daughter bypassing the security to enter this room." She said no longer talking directly to me.

"Excuse me, I'm over here and I don't know what you're talking about. I talked to the security and he told me to go that way because it would be faster when I was going to and from the cafeteria. It's a much easier route, by the way, I suggest you try it." I bullshitted.

"We're going to have to ask you to leave."

Usually when in this type of situation, my mom would come to my defense before I would have to start making up a story. But, as I was in my own argument with Tonya the nurse, my mom was having a battle herself. She was barely able to lift her head up, she was so physically and emotionally drained, at this point I realized this surgery was a lot more serious than I had originally thought. This wasn't a quick procedure, this was an extremely tedious surgery that would require months of recovery for her already frail body. She was also doing all this for me and the least I could give her was some peace and quiet.

"Alright, I'm leaving," I said back peddling on my original statement.

I began my walk of shame out of the recovery room, past the original nurse/bouncer and back to the waiting room.

The next few months, life began to work differently than I would have ever imagined. I had to come to terms with the fact that I was no longer a child. I would be in charge of myself essentially. Not entirely though, my mother would never relinquish that much control and I would forever have a bedtime. But, I was now equipped with a driver's license and would be taking care of my own errands. At 16 years old, it's a hard pill to swallow that you are no longer going to be babied.

I love the French!

## Freedom! Sike!

It was 1 am and I was dripping in sweat. I was on my 6th outfit change. I stood in front of the mirror and carefully scanned my all denim outfit. *Too Canadian,* I thought. I used the sleeve to wipe the sweat off my forehead. Tomorrow was my first day of college and I needed the perfect outfit that said both "I'm open to trying cocaine" and also "I was baptized" at the same time. I had one more hour before I could rinse off my St. Tropez mousse and go to sleep. I had to wake up in 5 hours in order to get to the orientation at 8 am sharp. I didn't want to be late and let all my new peers think that I was in the bathroom and missed my train.

David and I were staying at a relatives house on the outskirts of Paris. She worked in the development department at Chanel beauty and had given me some new products to test out. I planned on using them in front of my new friends to make them think I was more elegant than I was. In preparation for what I was calling my 'coming out' party, I had gone to a local nail salon and attempted to get a gel manicure. My French was hardly conversational at this point and I ended up accidentally getting black acrylics. I was too nervous to ask her to stop when I noticed she was gluing square pieces of plastic to each fingertip. So she continued and I left the salon looking 15% more Chola.

My mom and David were currently living in Annecy, only a 3 hour train ride away from Paris. My mom made me agree that I would call her three times a day and send her a photo of me in bed every night before I went to sleep. This was going to be my first time in my entire life that I was on my own. Actually, for most kids, attending college is the first time anyone was alone. But for me, it felt different. It wasn't so much living on my own and being able to do what I wanted whenever, it was more so the fact that I was no longer at the beck and call of my mom. She was now 3 hours away, which was still cause for alarm, but it would have to do for now.

After my tenth outfit change, I landed on a red, plaid skirt, knee-high black boots, a white t-shirt, and a black cardigan. It was a play on the Britney Spears *Hit Me Baby One More Time* music video outfit and I believed I nailed it.

"Are you ready to go?" David yelled up to my room from the kitchen.

"Coming!" I shouted as I hustled down the stairs.

"That's what you're wearing?" He asked giving me a once over. He didn't understand that looking like a Catholic school slut was my key to getting invited to the first big party of the year.

There was a Facebook group that my mom made me join prior to attending. It was meant to allow all the students to connect with each other and meet possible roommates. Instead, it ended up being an online marketplace for new students to sell drugs to other students without leaving their apartments. One student had posted that he was hosting a "dope ass rager" on the first Friday of orientation and to "send pics to get an invite."

David and I arrived in the 14th arrondissement of Paris at a dorm style building that was meant to hold students as we looked for apartments.

The walls were painted in all different bright colors to try to convince us subconsciously not to commit suicide. It had the opposite effect. As we pulled up in David's car and began to unload my five suitcases, I realized I was the only one who brought a parent.

I had to pretend like I didn't care that I was the only one with a chaperone because I was still pretending that I did not give a fuck about the American University of Paris and this was merely a layover on the way to NYU. The entire last year of high school I had been telling everyone that would listen that I would be attending NYU in the fall and I hadn't even applied yet. I had gotten the idea in my head, thanks to my mom telling me I was special my whole life, that I was exactly what that school was looking for. I knew they would look past my C average grades and lack of extracurriculars and see me for what I really was, amazing. I had written a killer essay that talked about my struggles of having a mom in a wheelchair and how hard it was not having naturally blonde hair in Southern California. I also threw in that I could almost run a 7 minute mile in case they were worried that I hadn't taken P.E. since 8th grade. But, when acceptance letters began to be sent out, mine must have gotten lost in the mail.

I ended up at the American University of Paris because it was the only college I got into. It was also the only application that I let my mom fill out on her own, so technically, she got in, not me. I had decided that I would reapply to NYU as a transfer student for the following year, hoping my year in Paris would make me stand out.

We walked to the front door where a senior was checking students in. I assumed he was a senior since he had a beard and was wearing a blazer. I was threatened and intimidated at the same time "Name?" He asked looking at his clipboard.

"Grace O'Connell."

He scrolled his finger down the piece of paper, "Ah, freshman.

Here is your orientation schedule Miss O'Connell." He handed me a booklet of papers from the table beside him.

"Miss O'Connell is my father, please call me Gracie."

David was more excited than I was to go through the instructions on how to get a French bank account and a list of all the bakeries walking distance from campus. Maybe he should have been the one to wear the slutty schoolgirl outfit. He played tennis, he had the legs for it.

After doing the mandatory lap of introductory booths, David decided that we were going to do this move our own way. He went ahead and set me up with a debit card and French phone plan under his already established accounts.

"I'm putting 100€ into the account to get it started, but after that, you have to deposit your own money." He said reluctantly handing me the shiny new card.

Later that afternoon David came with me to the cocktail mixer hosted in the basement of the temporary dorms. Again, he was the only parent. But I told him I needed him, I was too afraid to be left on my own. I hadn't established any connections with anyone I didn't want to immediately give a makeover to yet. We stood with our drinks at a table in the center of the room. A few people came over to chat and I realized everyone was just as nervous as I was. But David did all the talking for me anyways, which I was thankful for since I possessed the social skills of a serial killer. Since he was obviously fine on his own, I left David for a moment to find the bathroom.

"Your boyfriend is so nice. How did you guys meet?" I heard someone ask me. I turned around to find a girl who was only as tall as my nipples.

"Oh no that's not my... that's my dad." I said in disbelief and left the line.

David left after a few hours so I could branch out on my own. The first person I met was a boy named Joey. Joey was tall and skinny and I imagined we could share jeans if we ever needed to. He had one pierced ear which told me he was gay. I had always wanted a gay friend. I knew lesbians but I didn't have anything to talk to them about. Joey and I immediately bonded over our love of indie pop music and hatred of this mandatory mixer. We snuck out and took a cab over to the 1st arrondissement to get some absinthe at a cafe. I didn't know what absinthe was but I followed his lead, not wanting to out myself as a dork.

The absinthe came in what can only be described as a trough. This was my first time drinking alcohol that wasn't given to me by my mom at dinner or accidentally drank thinking Mikes Hard Lemonade was just lemonade.

After a few rounds, the conversation got quiet and I was able to realize something that will always be true to my heart, I love alcohol. I love it so much. Then I got dizzy.

I stood up from the sidewalk table and shouted, "Where is my convertible!??!"

I didn't have a convertible and couldn't remember actually ever riding in one before. Maybe it was time I went home. I got a cab and Joey explained to the driver where the dorm building was. He was already fluent in French so I decided he would be an important ally to have in this country.

When I arrived at my dorm room for the night, I noticed I still didn't have a roommate and that the room was spinning. I considered this a win and climbed into bed wearing only a bra and my retainer.

I had a dream that I flipped over in a canoe in shark infested water and woke up in a sweat the next morning. I sat up careful not to bonk my head on the top bunk that was above me and walked to the bathroom. I got ready for the day, slightly disappointed that I didn't have a roommate I could show my Chanel makeup to. I called my mom to tell her about my new friend Joey and how someone thought David was my boyfriend.

"Everything is going fine. I have an appointment with the housing office to get an apartment today." I said applying my third layer of mascara.

"What neighborhood are you looking at? You have to live somewhere near the Seine, it's too ugly on the outskirts. Try to find something in the 8th, it's the nicest." My mom suggested.

"I would love to live in the 8th, I just don't have the budget for that. I don't know how you think I'm going to find anything in a safe neighborhood for under 800€."

"There's plenty of studios for that price in those neighborhoods. You have to facetime me when you're at the apartments to show me."

"I don't think I'm going to find anything. I'm not gonna facetime you while the landlord is there, you'll cost me the apartment. They'll think I'm weird and can't live on my own."

"Have you met any royalty yet?"

"No, but I made a normal friend. And I tried absinthe."

I heard something rustling in my room. "Hold on I think this room has rats, I'll call you right back."

"Don't hang up on..." I hung up on her.

I put on the skirt I had hung on the shower door from yesterday and crept out into the room.

"Hello?" I said hoping the rat spoke English.

Instead of finding a rat rummaging through my sheets, there was a girl on the top bunk.

"Ahhhhghhh," I screamed and took a step back.

She reached over and grabbed her rectangular glasses. She looked exactly like one of The Rugrats cartoon characters.

After the initial shock wore off that I was in the same room as my favorite cartoon from childhood, she explained to me that she arrived at the orientation late and had climbed into the top bunk while I was fast asleep. And that she heard me get up in the middle of the night to barf. She was from Minnesota and this was her first time away from home. A good person would sympathize with her but I couldn't get over the way she pronounced her home state. She asked if I wanted to go to breakfast with her. Naturally, she already wanted to be my friend. My mom had warned me about getting single white femaled so I worried I would return later to her wearing my underwear.

"I can't. I have to go." I said leaving her alone with her accent.

Later that day, just as my mom had told me, I found an apartment. It was a sixth floor walk up studio with a bathroom the size of an airplane lavatory and kitchen that could barely fit one roasted chicken. I didn't mind the six flights of floors I would have to endure every day, I just fantasized about the calves they would give me. The building was above a Subway sandwich shop so the hallways always smelled like fresh bread and ham. The actual apartment was great though, dark wood floors, white walls, and all the appliances were brand new. The only furniture in the room was a pullout couch bed and a small wood desk. The bedding gave off the vibes that the previous owner had died in it, so I threw it off the balcony into the courtyard.

I face-timed my mom to show her my new apartment.

"You definitely need a rug. And I would just keep the bed out all the time and style it more like a daybed. Do you have your bedding and coffee table books yet?" She said over the phone.

"No, David is bringing me all my boxes tomorrow. I have to go back to the dorm to get my suitcases right now though."

"Ok take a cab, the sun is about to set."

I took a cab as advised back to the dorms. When I entered I found my temporary roommate, Katie, exactly where I left her. She was reading an anime comic book and eating a snickers, both she told me were brought from home.

It was 9 pm when I got to my apartment with my suitcases. I hadn't factored in how I would get all five bags up the stairs. I had the upper body strength of a cancer patient and little to no idea of how to install a rope pull. I called my new best friend Joey for assistance. He carried all five bags up the stairs and I opened a box of Oreos for him in exchange. As I unpacked, I realized that I had left my sheets in the boxes that David was bringing the next day and the only other bedding option was now being used as a birthing center for stray cats in the courtyard. I pulled out all the cashmere sweaters I had stolen from David and created a makeshift quilt for the night. Around 3 am I woke up and put on a scarf before returning to bed.

The next morning I had planned on picking up a few necessary items from Paris's version of a much more expensive Target, the BHV. I had 100€ in my bank account and was planning on spending all of it, plus the 4€ in coins I found in my pocket.

I called my mom for our first conversation of the day.

"I'm thinking about getting maybe just plain white sheets and a fun blanket. I decided I don't want the bedding I packed, it's so the old me."

"And who's the new you?" She asked.

"Someone who has plain white sheets and fun blanket!" I ran my hand over the 1000 thread count Egyptian cotton sheet set. I put them into my cart, eating up 70% of my budget.

"So I have to tell you something." My mom said hesitantly. This always meant bad news.

"Oh my god, what?"

"I'm moving to Paris next week!" She yelled as loud as she could through her breathing machine. Talking to her on the phone always made me forget that she was sick, until I heard the sounds of the air slipping from her nose.

"No, you are not! You can't do that to me! You can't follow me to college!" Her following me to college had always been a fear of mine and now it was happening. I paused waiting for her next sentence to be that she was enrolled in my film theory class as well.

Tears began to well up in my eyes. I sat down on a perfectly made example bed. "You can't always do what I do. I need to be on my own for once in my life."

"Relex drama queen, stop crying. I'm getting my own apartment and you only have to see me on weekends. Plus, you can come over and do laundry and I can take you out to dinner."

I began to warm up to the idea of being able to steal her jewelry whenever I needed to add a little oomph to an outfit. And in the back of my head, I knew it would be nice to have her around, but I wasn't about to tell her that. "Ok. But I'm not telling anyone you live here, and you can't live in my neighborhood."

"I don't want to live in your neighborhood."

I got off the phone call feeling deprived of this newfound freedom. I had only been on my own for three days and I was already accustomed to it. A grey striped cashmere throw caught my eye before I could burst into full tears. I added that to my cart too. I headed over to checkout, knowing very well I was 200€ over my budget but maybe something was on sale that I wasn't aware of.

I swiped my debit card and said a little prayer. It went through. Did David put more money on my card for me to spruce up my apartment? Did I have a salary that I wasn't aware of? Did I have a sugar daddy? I collected my purchases and headed towards the kitchen supplies.

Another 200€ worth of plates, cups and monogrammed dish rags went though. I felt like I was in the matrix. I checked the name on my card to make sure I hadn't unknowingly stolen someone else's identity. I took the escalator one floor down and got myself a gift card for later.

One week later, my mom had moved into an apartment walking distance from mine. I had finally started classes. I only had class for a few hours a day and only four days a week. I accidentally let this slip on a call with my mom and was forced to come over right then.

The moment I entered the apartment, David greeted me, "Hello douchebag. How was the BHV?"

"I don't know what you're talking about," I said playing dumb. My neck began to turn red from sheer nerves.

"You overdrafted your bank account 500€ you son of a bitch."

"I'm not a son of a bitch, I'm just a bitch."

He slowly explained to me the concept of overdrafting while cutting my card in half, "You owe me 500€."

Her apartment was much nicer than mine. It was a three-bedroom Haussman traditional style apartment with two fireplaces and a kitchen that had an oven, unlike mine. Any scammer worth her salt would have moved in with her and pocketed the rent money. But, I was relishing in my new found freedom. The past week I had been surviving off Diet Coke and potato chips that were chicken flavored and I loved every moment of it. I was able to have friends over without asking permission and could watch R rated movies with the volume all the way up. I got away with leaving wet towels on the floor and throwing away dishes if I didn't want to wash them. If I moved in with her, I would be a prisoner again, a prisoner with a view, but a prisoner nonetheless.

The originally agreed upon plan of only visiting my mom on the weekends was a good idea in theory, but there were some growing pains with her move plan. She didn't have steady caregivers in place, so I found myself spending the night at her apartment far more often than I would have liked. David was still in the process of catching up to my mom's sporadic move and had to take a few more trips back to Annecy to get the rest of their things. My mom complained that he was going slower than he had to because he wanted his alone time. She probably was right.

I was over at my mom's house one night for dinner when she picked a fight with David over buying the wrong type of almond milk.

"I'm going to divorce you!" my mom threatened.

"Not if I divorce you first!" David yelled back from the living room.

"If you guys get divorced, do I still have to pay you back?" I interrupted.

"YES!" They both shouted from separate rooms.

A few moments of silence passed and we all went back to watching different TVs in different rooms. I watched The Girls Next Door with my anxiety in full force. I didn't know how I was going to pay David back, getting a job was out of the question. Why didn't he tell me that I could go over my limit? Technically, this wasn't my fault.

"Daaavviid, help me!" My mom yelled from her bedroom a few moments later.

David jumped up and ran into the room. "What? What's wrong now?" He asked thinking she was just going to ask him to click the button to go to the next episode of Real Housewives of New York City.

"I think I'm having a heart attack."

Within 5 minutes, we could hear the ambulances outside the apartment. I sat down next to my mom and tried to calm her down. I never would have guessed that a heart attack would be the thing to kill her. David went to open the door for the emergency responders. Five husky paramedics and two equally sexy firefighters walked in. I ran to the bathroom to freshen up.

They conducted a series of tests on her and questioned where the pain was coming from.

"My heart just feels like it's beating out of control and my left arm is numb. Everything is tight."

They continued to look for the source of this pain but came up empty handed. It was suggested that they take her in the ambulance to the hospital.

"I am not going there! That's where they killed Princess Diana!" My mom was a firm believer that if the Parisian hospital had better equipment, we wouldn't have had to put up with Camila Parker Bowels as much.

David anxiously paced around the room and began to refold the stack of sweaters in the closet. I could see him from across the room pulling his phone out. I received his text 2 minutes later.

"You owe me 500€ even if mom dies. Love David."

The paramedics pulled him aside to chat while I got back up in bed next to my mom.

"Lean in I have to tell you something." My mom said quietly.

"You're going to be ok. People have heart attacks all the time." I waited for her to tell me her deathbed secrets. There was one, in particular, I was aiming for.

She once told me she dated a guy for a few months in LA in the early 90's. He had a big Hollywood Hills house but it wasn't clear what he did to pay for it. He let her have free reign of the house but told her there was one room she couldn't go in because it was private. He left her alone at the house one night and naturally, she went into the room. It was a large library style room with a museum-like case in the center. She went up close to the glass, there was a small violin inside it with the initials "A.H." on the base. The plaque below described in detail that the violin was Adolf Hitler's. She left the next day and never spoke to him again. He later went on to be a successful actor, but she wouldn't tell me who because she knew I would report it to TMZ.

"Was Ben Affleck the Nazi?" I whispered into her ear.

"No. But that's not what I want to tell you." She paused. "I'm faking all this, don't tell David?"

I was stunned, "You don't really have ALS?"

"No, I'm not really having a heart attack. I just wanted some attention."

Eliot and my mom sharing a smoke.

## The Kris To My Kylie

On my first day of class at the American University of Paris, I met Eliot from Nebraska. They had long dark hair and wore knee-high lace-up Doc Martins. We had an immediate connection over our love of swearing and Romana Singer. By the following spring, there wasn't a day we weren't together. I was living in a studio by myself and they had a roommate that moonlighted as a DJ, so we decided that it would be in both of our best interests to live together.

We had found our apartment through our school's version of a rental agency. There was a large selection of apartments with questionable landlords, but you didn't have to pay a deposit. Eliot and I spent countless hours ixnaying apartments for reasons such as "the mood just doesn't feel right" and "I don't want to live *that* close to the metro." We finally landed on an apartment that we both agreed was nice enough to live in but not nice enough that we could destroy it. We also loved it because the living room was painted lavender and there was a fireplace.

Fresh off our flights from the U.S., we pulled up to the apartment in an 80€ cab. For two students with no income, we should have learned how to take the bus. The building was above a tabac which normally would cause anyone to rethink their living arrangements, but for us, it was exciting. We now had a bar and cigarette shop that stayed open until 2 am.

After buzzing the apartment 5A, we were let in and immediately were immersed in our new neighborhood. The ground floor apartment kept their door open all day because the window to the street wouldn't open. They also slow cooked lamb tikka masala all day. Again, another sign we were in heaven. I made a mental note to send them a fruit basket as a way to gain an invite to their nightly dinners.

Our landlord walked down the stairs and greeted us. She was tall, blonde, German and disappointed. She told us to leave our bags and come up to do the walk through so she can leave.

"When I offered this apartment for rent with the university, I assumed you would be French students. Are you Americans?" She asked graciously gliding up the stairs. There was an elevator but she didn't want to be in a small space with us and I didn't blame her.

"Who told you we were American?" I asked trying to hide my neck pillow.

Eliot and I both were sweating and wearing sweats, something our landlord wasn't used to. My hair was still stuck to the side of my face from the nap I took in the cab and we both smelled like mayonnaise from the kebab we grabbed for the unpacking.

"Follow me, please. You can come back for your belongings when we are done with the lease." She said pointing at our eight suitcases.

"I don't think we should leave the bags down here, why don't you two go up and I'll stay with the bags." Eliot offered.

"Very good, I'll bring the elevator key down in a moment." She said not pausing from her walk up the stairs.

"The elevator needs a key?" I asked. Elevator keys were usually reserved for penthouse suites and all signs pointed to the obvious, this was no penthouse.

"Yes, it's so the guests of the residents do not have access to it. There are a lot of guests here." She said effortlessly. I was panting and we were only on floor three.

After the key was brought down, the landlord began to show me around. The apartment was adorable. It was spacious as well. There was a large living room with a fireplace, two bedrooms with queen sized beds, a small updated kitchen, and a long and narrow bathroom. The apartment even had its own toilet, which is something to be thankful for in Paris.

All the furniture was great too, a leather Eames style chair, glass dining table, and oriental rugs. But, when I entered one of the bedrooms, there was a piece about the size of half a twin bed, covered in a white sheet. I was about to ask what it was when I received a phone call. It was Eliot.

"Hey, where are you?" I asked.

"Listen, I broke the elevator. I don't know what happened but don't tell the Nazi." Eliot was attempting to jam open the glass elevator door in the background.

"What do you mean you broke the elevator? Like are you stuck in it?"

"No I'm not in it, but our bags are. I tried to send the elevator up without me since it's the size of a sport tampon. But then it was working and suddenly stopped and now it's in between the ground floor and the first floor."

"I think they call the ground floor the first floor here actually."

"Doesn't matter, can you come help me?"

"Yeah but I don't know what I can do to help, you're smarter than me."

The German walked into the bedroom where I was, "Is everything good?"

"Yeah yeah, the elevator is having a wee bit of an issue." I tried to mix in some Bristish vocab to throw her off the fact that I was American.

Without saying a word, she walked out of the apartment and down the stairs. I followed her closing the door behind me.

"Ah yes, you see you must be inside the elevator for it to move, you confused the elevator and it will not move unless someone is inside to push the button." The landlord said pointing out the obvious.

"Yeah, I can see that now. Is there a way to call it back down?" Eliot replied.

"No, you must call the operator, let me get the phone number inside the apartment." She pushed past me to run back up the stairs.

Eliot and exchanged looks of terror before I followed the landlord back up the apartment. It was only 10 am and I had already hit my 10,000 steps just from these fucking stairs.

"You should not have closed the door." She said as I reached the landing. "It is now locked. We are locked out."

This particular door did not have a knob like a traditional door. The key inserted acts as a knob when you turn it. We were now locked out of the elevator, the apartment, and our landlord's heart.

"I must call my husband to bring the spare set to let you in. I have an appointment very soon, so I do not have time to show you everything anymore, you must mail me the signed portion of the lease."

I simply nodded along, fearful that if I said the wrong thing, we would lose the lease all together.

"Enjoy the apartment, my husband will be here in an hour. The number for the elevator repair is in the booklet on the dining table. You must fix the elevator today." She said reaching her hand out to shake mine and then departed.

I heard her say goodbye to Eliot on the ground floor. Once it was confirmed she was out of the building, I went back downstairs.

"I got us locked out," I said taking a seat on the floor.

"Do you think she's going to take a hit out on us?" Eliot asked.

"No, that's the mafia. She's going to do much worse, she's German."

An hour later, her husband arrived and let us in the apartment. He was much more friendly than his wife and even offered to stay to help us with the elevator repairman. Maybe he wasn't German or maybe it was because he was a pedofile, either way, we decided that we would call him with any issues rather than his wife.

Upon entering the apartment, I pointed out the piece of furniture that was covered with a sheet.

"That wasn't in the photos."

We walked up to it slowly, like we were ghost hunters. Once the sheet was removed, a metal medical table was revealed. It was very obviously the table they used in a morgue, the table with the bodies and the toe tags.

"Aw fuck," Eliot whispered.

We decided to move the table/final resting place to the living room. The first few months living there, we had it covered with a tablecloth in an attempt to disguise it as an actual table. We then had to remove the table cloth when red wine was spilled on it. After that, we just embraced it, with the right decorative accents, it almost looked like a Restoration Hardware piece. But, we knew the truth, this is where the German woman had stored her great grandfather's body, Mr. Adolf Hitler himself.

The apartment began to show it's true colors more and more every day. A different appliance died on us every month, floor boards began to come up, and the lovely lavender paint had begun to peel.

By August the following year, we were down to one burner and the bathroom sink. We were too scared of our landlords to ever call in with repairs. If you haven't been to France in August, don't. They don't believe in air conditioning nor deodorant, which when combined, can be lethal.

"Are you also sweating from your butt crack?" I rolled over from my back to my stomach on the floor and looked at Eliot for answers. The floor was the coldest spot in the apartment, I had even taken to sleeping on it a few times, usually by accident.

"Yeah, and it's called swamp ass." They replied.

"I just got another email from Wells Fargo, my balance is now at negative fifteen US dollars. What is that in euros?" I was now topless and starfishing on the ground. The apartment only had one fan so we traded off every hour using it.

"I think it's like 10€, so you're not in as much debt as you thought." They replied while taking off her pants. "My bank account was closed."

"That's ok, we have almost twenty euros in coins saved up. All of this has been stressing me out so much, I should get a job." I had a well paying job as an assistant to a fashion editor the semester prior, but the 5 am wake up calls were taking a toll on my bar hopping schedule. "Or actually, do you want to go to Spain?"

A family friend had a house on the island of Mallorca. Her name was Diandra and she was fabulous. She co-owned almost half the island with her ex-husband, Micheal Douglas. They bought it together back in the 80's and had spent years transforming it into a private paradise. There were about 10 small guest houses around the property, so when you stayed there, you didn't have to interact with anyone until 8 pm if you wished. I had spent many summers there as a kid with my mom, even one time, staying there for two months by ourselves.

During the summer, the house had an open invitation policy. You could just show up and there would be a guest house ready for you with a bottle of house wine on the bedside table.

"We can book the tickets on the Amex my dad gave me," Eliot

said.

One week later, we were out of our sauna of an apartment and on our way to pretend to be rich for a week.

The drive from the airport to the house is about an hour of twisting and turning up and over a one lane mountain road. When you finally reach the first gate of the property, you are greeted by roaming donkeys leading the way. I stuck my arm out of the window to pet the smallest one on the face. He immediately sneezed on me.

We unloaded our bags from the car and were led to our private house. It overlooked the ocean on one side and had a terrace on the other side, facing the mountain we had just driven over. If you were going to write the next great American novel, it would be here. On the table on the patio, there was the expected bottle of wine, a pack of welcome cigarettes and a handwritten note that dinner was at 9 pm. The room was large and cold, this was the only place in Europe with central A/C.

We had about four hours to kill before dinner, so we strolled the property. We walked through the vineyards and picked grapes off the vines to snack on. We dipped our feet in the pool and were greeted by the chef with watermelon juice cocktails and olives. I started practicing my phone call to my mom to let her know I was dropping out of school and never coming back.

It was now 8:30 pm and we still hadn't seen Diandra. Eliot and I walked into the kitchen to have dinner. On the table were individual bowls of gazpacho with our initials drawn in creme fraiche, homemade paella and all the Iberico ham in the world. As we were sitting down, Diandra walked in with her three children, Imara, Hawk and Hudson, and her boyfriend Paolo. We discussed the plan for the week and that there was no plan. We were free to do whatever we wanted, whenever.

"The only thing I was thinking is one day we can take the boat over to that little restaurant on the cliff and go swimming," Diandra said casually. The restaurant was a small seafood restaurant that overlooked the Mediterranean ocean and the only way to get there was by boat.

As we were getting ready for bed that night, I stared at myself in the beautiful 17th century gold gilt mirror. A few months ago, I ordered one of Kylie Jenner's lip kits, in the hopes that I could fool someone into thinking I had lips. It wasn't working, because now I was looking at a mouth that looked like I had just eaten a fudgesicle. There was a dark brown lining around my mouth, the rest of the lipstick had been licked off at dinner. The dark brown color also wasn't the best choice, I probably should have gone with Tutti Fruity.

"Does this look natural?" I asked walking out of the bathroom holding a finger on the top and bottom of my lips, trying to stretch them out.

"Oh my god, I want lip injections too," Eliot replied and did the same.

"Would you actually?" I asked, never have even considered actually getting my lips done.

My lips have been a sore spot ever since two weeks ago. I noticed that when I smiled, my top lip would curl under, showing off my small square teeth. I didn't know lip injections were a thing people outside the Real Housewives franchise actually did until Kylie Jenner admitted to it. She's not that far outside the Real Housewives world, but she was enough, convincing for me to actually start to consider the injections. I would just have to get over my fear of needles and maybe get a job to pay for them.

I let go of my hold on my upper lip and got into bed. Our bed for the week was a California King, Diandra must have shipped it in. All of my beds in all of my apartments were not even real mattresses, they were the top layer of a futon. I hadn't slept this well since high school.

We woke up refreshed and ready for a grueling day of lounging by the pool and taking photos of ourselves. This process repeated every day for a week.

The day before it was time to head back to Paris, we took the boat to the restaurant. On our way there, we anchored in the middle of the sea. Everyone immediately got into the water. It was so warm it felt like a bath. I started to pee. Peeing in the ocean is the best feeling, nothing feels more free. Eliot and I swam far away from the boat, there was nothing to be scared of in this water because you could see all the way to the ocean floor. I used my life jacket to float on top of and began to cry.

I didn't know if it was because I hated my lips or because my mom wasn't here to enjoy this with me. The last time I had been here, was with my mom, years before we even knew what ALS was. My mom was the woman who was scared of the wind. Everything made her fear for her life and mine. But, in Mallorca, she was a new woman. It might have been all the salt and wine she was ingesting, but here, she was fearless. She jumped off cliffs into the ocean, she drove a Vespa, she puked at a farmer's market. She was her best self here and it was one of the first times I felt a pain that wasn't for me, but for her instead.

The instances before this, I would cry about what was being taken away from me, my mom. I hadn't once stopped and consider what was being taken away from her. Not only her life, but her freedom. She no longer was the woman she had been, nor the woman she wanted to be. She had plans for herself once she was done raising my dumb ass. She was going to buy an old chateau in the south of France and live out of her Under The Tuscan Sun dreams finally. But all that was taken away with three small letters.

As I sat in the Mediterrain ocean and cried, I didn't understand how I could be so happy yet so sad at the same time.

I splashed some water on my face to disguise my crying as just a sunburn. I didn't want now to be the moment I had a breakdown. My mom wouldn't want that, she would want me to live the life she couldn't live. I was going to jump off that cliff and I was going to try calamari.

Eliot and I arrived back in Paris and were greeted with a thick cloud of French B.O. French B.O. Is stronger than American B.O. because of all the brie inhaled. After dropping off my bags at our apartment, I left for the metro to head over to my mom's apartment.

The walk to the metro from my apartment was just about 2 blocks, but those two blocks were picked up out of Syria and assembled here. I crossed the street to what I deemed the safer side when I saw a man crouching between two parallel parked cars. He was holding onto each car as if he was trying to support himself. I walked towards him, thinking something was wrong like he had fallen or maybe was stabbed. As I got closer, I realized that he was pooping. On the street. In the morning. I wasn't in Mallorca anymore.

I arrived at my mom's beautiful apartment near the Louvre. I wouldn't find anyone pooping over here.

"I saw a man pooping on my street," I exclaimed loudly as I walked in.

"Do you want to move in with me?" She asked. This would make all her dreams come true, I bet she didn't think a hobo poop would be the reason why though.

"Actually maybe." I sat on the chair across from her bed. "If I move in with you, can I get lip injections?"

"You don't need lip injections. Plus, they're dangerous."

"I would look so much better with them though. My face is designed for big lips, I don't have any hard features, pillowy lips would complete my bone structure."

"Pillowy lips? No, you don't need them."

"I would just feel so much more confident in my own skin if I had them."

"Why are you saying that? Did someone tell you you had small lips, because thin lips are beautiful. Just look at Farrah Faucet."

"She's dead!"

We went back and forth until it was my mom's nap time. Every thin lipped beauty she named was from the 70's and no longer relevant. Big lips were the new big boobs. I reminded her that she got a boob job to confirm for society so why couldn't I do the same. The conversation ended on a maybe.

I repeated my visits daily to her apartment on a quest, a quest for plump lips. I think I wore her down because one day she agreed. I was 20 years old at the time so technically I didn't need her permission, but I did need her to spot me. Just like Kris Jenner did for Kylie. Except, my mom and I were more a Jonbenet and Patsy Ramsey pair. I wish she didn't die so we could do that as a couples costume for Halloween.

The day of the appointment came and I decided to bring David. I needed someone who could translate "I want to look like Shilo Jolie-Pitt," to French. I laid down on the table that looked almost identical to the morgue table in my apartment, except this one had leather padding.

The doctor and David spoke for a while as they pointed and touched my lips. This was now out of my hands. I had watched videos of lip injections on Youtube prior so I would know what I would be in for. I had also taken two Xanax on the cab ride over in preparation. I felt relaxed and ready.

Then the doctor began. This was a different procedure than what I had watched. She poked two small needle holes on either side of my mouth then threaded a small plastic needle like device all the way across my top lip and again across my bottom lip. I couldn't tell if it was me sweating or David, as he was about 2 inches away from my forehead. The room started to go white.

I have a tendency to pass out. I passed out when I got my ears pierced, then again when I got them repierced, once when I got my hair cut too short, and most recently during a pap smear.

I woke up to smelling salts.

"Is it done?" I asked opening my eyes.

"No, you passed out and she had to stop," David said stroking my face.

"Why didn't you tell her to finish while I was out?" I blubbered through my swollen lips.

The doctor went back in for seconds.

"Wow wow what, what is she doing?" I didn't think my body could physically hold anymore Juvederm.

"It's for the cupid's bow," David said gesturing towards the center of my top lip. When did he learn what a cupid's bow was?

I gave her the go ahead to continue, I had come this far, I wasn't about to pussy out now. She added a few more injections to my top lip and then massaged them for 10 minutes. That was my favorite part.

We left the office and I passed out again. We walked to the corner store and bought me a Coke to get my blood sugar pumping again. I tried to take a sip, but my numb lips wouldn't let me. It was like I had two two cocktail weiners instead of lips. I tilted my head back and tried to pour the Coke down my throat but the carbonation just made it come back up. I really wanted a Coke but my body wasn't letting me.

All that pain was worth it though, I finally felt like my face was the way it was supposed to be. My lips were perfect and I couldn't wait to show them off. I went to Sephora on the way home and bought a red lipstick. Even though the injections were hardly noticeable in size, I finally felt confident. It's amazing what a few CC's can do for your self-esteem.

Eliot and I threw a party in honor of my new lips but told the guests it was to celebrate the new school year. But because of all the Xanax I had taken, I went to bed early and missed the whole thing.

The next morning I woke up and looked in the mirror. I looked like

I had been put through a meat grinder. There was dried blood on my teeth and two bruises forming on either side of my mouth. I spotted an open can of Coke on the kitchen counter. I grabbed it with triumph and took a sip to wash out the taste of blood. Our kitchen sink wasn't working and I didn't believe that sink water from the bathroom was drinkable. As the soda hit my tongue, I realized that there was something floating in my mouth. It was a cigarette. I opened my mouth and let the butt and soda roll down my chest. Someone had put out a cigarette in this can, and it was now it was inside me. Before I could even process what to do next, I vomited. Right down the front of my shirt, like a baby.

I quickly walked to the bathroom mirror and looked at myself in disgust. I had someone else's used cigarette stuck in my cleavage, vomit dripping off my chin and there was still blood in my teeth. At least I had lips though. Maybe it was time I moved into my mom's.

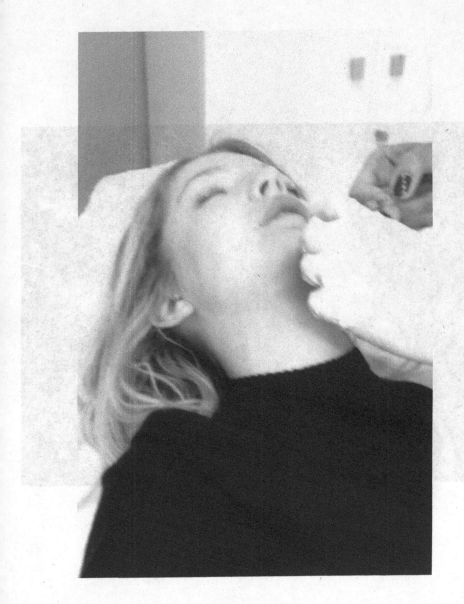

Getting new lips.

Getting new lips.

# The War On Terror Gave Me Anxiety

I was six years old when 9/11 happened, so I don't remember it much. I was living on Balboa Island in Orange County in a perfect beach house with my Mom and step-dad John. The house had old wood floors downstairs and sisal carpet upstairs. I didn't like the way the sisal would leave imprints on my knees, making them itch, so I rarely was in my room. Plus, the TV was downstairs.

Every morning before school I would sit on the floor of the living room, eat a bowl of Captin' Crunch and watch TV. One Tuesday morning, things were different though. I bounced downstairs ready to watch Spongebob Squarepants before I had to get dressed for school. My mom and John were sitting on the couch watching the news in silence.

My mom didn't even try to shield me from watching because it didn't feel real. Two planes had hit the twin towers. The events on the television were so graphic I thought they were watching a movie. My mom left the room to make some phone calls. I took her seat on the couch and watched in a trance.

"My dad just said they're expecting L.A. to be the next target, we have to get out of here." My mom said walking back into the room.

"Relax, we don't live in L.A," John replied calmly. It was strange that they were married since John was so level headed and my mom was insane.

"We can't let Gracie go to school today, we have to stay at home."

"I have to go to work but you two can stay here." He said standing up and facing the TV again, "This is just unbelievable."

Watching 2000 people die on live TV as a child might have altered the way my generation lives today. Anxiety is a problem that almost all people my age deal with daily. We might not have grown up with serial killers like our parents did, but we understood that terrorism wasn't just something people say to scare you, it was real.

My mom kept me home from school that day and the day after. If she had her way, I would have started homeschooling at that very moment. L.A. was never hit.

14 years later, I was living on my own in Paris, anxiety still intact. I wasn't exactly on my own though, my mom's apartment was close enough that I could roll my laundry basket over on the weekends.

One afternoon, I went over for my usual date that ended with me stealing half of her groceries. Just as I was reaching for the rotisserie chicken, she yelled out to me. I didn't understand how she knew I was stealing the chicken, but I didn't put it past her.

"I'm moving to Provence!!" She shouted in excitement as I entered her bedroom.

"Whuh?" This news hit me right on the forehead, leaving a now noticeable red spot.

"I just signed the lease on a house." Ever the delight, she had decided at her own will, that this move was already official. I don't even recall a prior conversation about moving to Provence ever taking place. She had mentioned that she wanted to move to the South of France a few times but she had also mentioned that she wanted to be single and childless in that same conversation, so I thought she was just listing the impossible.

"Listen, I know your game. I know you cannot hold a pen, so Joel signed for you, technically making this all fraudulent." I replied. Her caregivers were her accomplices on all her fraud and Joel was no better. He was four feet tall and of Filipino descent. His height was the main reason my mom hired him immediately as his caregiver, his cute round cheeks were a close second.

"We're going next month and you can come every weekend to visit," she said.

"First of all, no," I replied. Then I paused.

"...and second of all?" she asked, expecting there to be another reason.

"I'm thinking," I said and left the room to heat up my new favorite snack, which was France's answer to a hot pocket.

"Why do you think this is a good idea? You know David can't move down there. People are going to think that you're separating. Do you want everyone to think you cheated on him? Because that's what people are going to think." The fact that she couldn't physically cheat on him was lost on me. They only way she could cheat was if she was molested by a doctor.

She explained the routine that would be put into place for her move. She would have her two caregivers, Joel and Victor, each work a few days and then switch. Joel and Victor were both adorable and I always felt bad when my mom undermined their medical skills and overestimated their design skills. They were there to make sure she stayed alive, she thought they were there to fung shui the living room. They both lived in Pairs but this was not one of her concerns. She would employ a nurse to make routine visits during the day for bathroom breaks. Going to the bathroom was no longer a one man job, not even a two man job, but now a three man job. Perhaps if any of the men had a little more upper body strength, the count would go back to two. Or if my mom lost a few pounds, she looked like she was anorexic but weighed like she had just won Nathan's Hot Dog Eating Contest of Coney Island.

Within the month, my mom had left her Paris apartment along with her entourage and with as many suitcases that could be tied to her wheelchair as possible. She had rented a house that was honestly adorable. It was a stone cottage with a matching pool and poolhouse. There was a long pea gravel driveway and rose bushes everywhere. Even someone like me who prefers carpet and updated kitchens could appreciate the quaintness of her new house. The only problem was that it was winter. It was cold and grey and nothing was open.

The house also did not have an actual address. I'm not sure how this was possible, but I'm going to blame the Greeks on this one. No mail ever got delivered and when the internet would go out from it raining too hard, you couldn't get anyone over to repair it. No one could find you there. It was a great house for an escaped convict with an appreciation of shabby chic, but for someone who needed to be found by the paramedics, not so much.

I had been visiting almost every weekend, but since I had class on Friday and Monday, it was usually just a 24 hour visit. So when I told my mom that I had four days off in November, she immediately booked me a train ticket.

She had moved there only about a month before but the house was already under construction. This was a rental, but that never stopped her. She had already recovered the mix and match tiling with sisal (a staple of hers), painted the accent walls white and thrown out all the furniture the house came with. She was transforming this place into the quintessential Provence farmhouse, minus the farm. There was a large pool out front that I couldn't wait to swim in without anyone seeing me. Too bad it was

November.

November in Provence is a slow time. The Christmas decorations aren't up yet and it's too cold to really be outside comfortably.

My first day of my fall break, I was woken up at 7 am by my mom's caregiver, "We're leaving for the flea market in 20 minutes." He told me through the crack in the door.

My mom had told me about this plan the night before. I ignored her because I assumed she would change her mind the next day. I had known my mom for 20 years and still didn't understand that she never cancels on a flea market.

A flea market in Provence is like nothing else in the world. The air smells fresher yet like the dusty past at the same time. My mom had started an online shop selling antiques she acquired from all around France, so this was technically a business trip.

This wasn't a new venture for my mom though. All her life she had been selling antiques, she was just doing it in a new body now. In 2002, my mom opened up a small booth inside of an antique market. Usually, these booths are treated like a storage unit, where people will visit once a month and haphazardly throw all the things they don't want and try to make a quick buck. But not my mom, she would not be treating it as her own personal garage sale. She painstakingly collected antiques and staged the booth and was the only one in the whole market that actually stayed at her booth 5 days a week. After that, she gained some loyal clients who would hire her to be their interior decorator. This business didn't last too long because she hated being told what to do and all her clients had no style. She would come home from shopping with a client and complain that they "didn't understand why British flags as fabric were not chic, they were cheap." She then opened up a store called Circa in Montecito with my grandma. They went on a buying trip to Paris to fill up their three story store before opening day. This store was an immediate hit with the locals, they paid their rent within 20 minutes of opening the door. When the store closed its doors in 2009, my mom and I moved to NYC. She filmed a pilot for a design show with Diandra, but then they got in a huge fight and the show was canceled before it was even picked up. Then something called ALS got in the way, well not really actually. Even being paralyzed from the neck down, she still managed to create and grow a successful business, all from the comfort of her voice-operated computer. I can't even tie my shoes yet she was traveling around Europe on the hunt for antiques in a wheelchair.

Every two weeks, she would visit a flea market and purchase her goods for her monthly sale. After making her selections, she taught her caregivers to take product shots and measure each item. She would then write descriptions and brief historical information on every piece and upload it to her website. This wasn't her only job though, she also had a blog, which is probably where you know her from. She would publish a blog every week, whether it was a good week or a bad week, she would write about it and hold nothing back.

Watching her confess every emotion and every thought she had to thousands of people every week made me want to be more like her. Be more vulnerable. Be stronger. Instead, I mocked her for having a blog at all. "You're not a teenage girl," I would tell her.

This particular sale would focus on all the charms found in the south of France. She was shopping for the perfect pieces that would fit into a home in America that represented Provence without being kitschy. There's a fine line between the two, a poster of a boulangerie is not the answer.

This was the first sale that I ever really helped out on, and the first one I started to express some interest in. I was also promised a Chanel scarf if I helped out. Going through a French woman's trash, you're bound to find some treasures. It takes a very particular eye to be able to do this, and my mom was the master. She would find pieces that I would have gone right past and then bargain the price down to half of what they were asking for, the wheelchair might have helped.

Once we got home from Mecca, she had me arrange her purchases to set a little scene for Instagram.

"No no, the Chinoiserie box goes in the front." She wasn't able to use her arms so pointing would not be an option. Words only. "No, not that front."

I never did it right and would then complain that she was just going to have to trust me. She shouldn't have had to trust me to do the work for her, she should be doing this herself, but she couldn't. She physically couldn't do what she loved anymore and I was a real bitch about it.

"Can I take my break now?" I asked.

"No, you already had your 15 minutes." She said seriously. She ran this online startup like a Fortune 500. I couldn't wait until I was hired full time, then I could finally qualify for paid time off.

After about 45 minutes of arranging six small pieces, we then had to wait for the light to be just so. I would snap the picture and run back into her room for approval. She was allowed nap breaks during a shoot because she was the boss.

"Just fluff up the feathers on the helmet a little bit more, then it's good."

I ran back to the setup, fluffed the helmut feathers and took the final shot. We then would sit for 30 minutes going back and forth about a caption and the hashtags and what time to post. Most of her customers were U.S. based, so we would have to calculate the time difference, which always added another 10 minutes onto our total.

We would repeat this situation every time she had a sale. I was deemed her Instagram guru which was strange because she had more followers than me. I think my age helped me get the job, I was her diversity hire. We wrapped up the day at 8pm, just in time for a charcuterie plate. The best part about the Provence flea markets is that we would stop at an open-air market on the way home. All the cheese and meat you could dream of. I usually stick to prosciutto and parmesan since my palette has still not been refined.

I was finally laying in bed alone watching TV when I got an alert text from my school.

There had been a shooting in Paris.

I jumped up and went to my mom's room.

"Turn on the news," I said to David. I loved saying that phrase, made me sound like I wasn't just watching "TLC presents Hoarders" in the other room. "There was a shooting in Paris."

David changed the channel from Bravo to the BBC. The shooting was much larger than I had thought. A few months earlier, there was a terrorist attack at the office of the French newspaper, Charlie Hebdo over political cartoons that depicted Mohammad. That attack shook Paris because unlike in America, mass murder is something that doesn't happen every week. This one was 10 times larger.

I had only gotten the news five minutes before and there were already 50 people dead. The details were coming in slowly, but as we watched the live footage, I started to recognize the venue. It was a concert hall that I had visited a few times during my Freshman year. I immediately went to the selfish thought we all have during a tragedy, it could have been me.

An update came across the screen, there was another attack, this time only a few blocks away at a restaurant I had visited the week before. It was also on the same street as my apartment.

I began to receive panicked texts from people asking if I was in Paris. Thank god I wasn't. I passed that restaurant every day on my way to the metro. It was a traditional French cafe that wasn't very good but was convenient and always packed with people.

After watching a few moments of live coverage of people running away from the scene, another update came across the screen. A third location had been targeted. Then another, then another. I soon learned that while I was busy with my charcuterie earlier in the night, there had been a first attack at a stadium right outside Paris during a soccer game, or excuse me, a football game. The death count began to rise on the bottom of the screen, it was almost at 100 people so far.

Everyone in the room got quiet and watched the massacre unfold live. I couldn't get the thought out of my head that I could have been there. I often resort to the butterfly effect state of mind during an event like this. If my mom would have not moved to Provence, I would have stayed in Paris during this break from class. I probably would have gone out that night to a local bar or restaurant. I would have been in my neighborhood. I would have been dumb and gone towards the commotion. But, my mom didn't live in Paris, and I wasn't in Paris, I was far away from everything that was going on.

I began to almost wish I was there, to see what was happening with my own eyes. I slapped myself on the stomach to shake myself out of my quest to be apart of the action. I needed to be thankful that I wasn't there.

I fell asleep in my mom's bed that night, scared of the photos I would Google if I were alone.

The next morning the TV was still tuned into the news. 130 people were dead, 400 more injured. I was supposed to return home that afternoon but changed my train ticket to Monday. I was scared. The hunt for the remaining attackers was still underway, I worried they would be hiding in my empty apartment.

I left on Tuesday morning with David and went straight to class. My school had ramped up security since there were talks that such a prominent American University could be a target next. My school was also surrounded by Ambassador's homes. The entire neighborhood of the seventh was being patrolled by G.I. Joes with machine guns strapped to their chest, two of them were positioned outside my school's main building.

The next week, a metal fence was built in front of the courtyard of my school's cafe. It was actually a bar, but we were supposed to refer to it as a cafe. Students could no longer leisurely stroll in and out of the building for smoke breaks. We now had to scan our ID's and have our bags checked before entering the building. Even with all the new security, students were feeling less safe than before. It felt like a fortress, not a liberal arts school. It actually felt like the public high school I went to in NYC for a few months, except less JAPs.

People began to seriously consider transferring. I even considered transferring to somewhere in New York or California, somewhere that wasn't under Marshall law. My grandparents encouraged me coming home, my mom was the voice of reason and told me to stay. Usually, she would be the first to fear for my safety, but she knew America wasn't any more safe.

I didn't actually want to leave Paris, I just enjoyed being dramatic. Every time I walked past the cafe that had been part of the attack, I lifted a hand to my forehead and whispered "Oh mon dieu," before taking a bite of my croissant.

Every sound made me jump after the attacks. I would wake up when I heard people in the hallways, sure they were there to get me. I began placing a chair until the door handle as an added method of security. I would sit for hours in the dark, looking out the window, just looking for anything suspicious. The entire next month, I avoided the metro.

I began chatting with a weird student who was known for roofy-ing girls. I overheard him giving out tips about how to survive a terrorist attack. I figure getting roofied was better than being shot, so I pulled up a chair and listened.

"You're going to want to either be in the first cab or the last cab, never the middle. If there is going to be an attack on the metro, they're going to blow up the middle cart. These guys will always be freshly shaven, it's part of their ritual, but sometimes, they have a beard. They will be wearing bulky clothing. like coats and jackets, that's why there's not as many attacks in the summer, it's harder to hide their suicide vests. But, they also know how to hide them, so also look out for guys in just larger t-shirts." He continued on with his nonsense as I got up and left.

The only advice I took and still follow to this day was never riding in the center cab on the metro, but it was hard to look out for everyone in every season as he advised. I found myself getting off the metro, many stops before mine from an overwhelming sense of doom.

I moved out of my apartment and into another one a week later. But the insanity inside my mind did not stop, I was certain there was going to be another terrorist attack aimed especially for me. It wasn't helping that I had a friend who interned for the American Embassy and told me every day, "I can't say anything, but be prepared."

Be prepared for what? When is it happening? Should I buy a gun? I became obsessed with peeing every time I saw a toilet, afraid that if the attack, that was apparently imminent, happened when I least expected it, that I would pee my pants.

Peeing my pants had already happened once that year at a Monoprix grocery store and I was going to do everything in my power to prevent that from happening again.

Christmas break came and went and nothing had happened except for me stocking up on canned goods in preparation for the rapture. I was busy turning into a full blown doomsday preparer that I didn't even see what was happening in my own home. My own personal terrorist was moving back to Paris.

# What I Saw Outside My Front Door In The 10th Arrondisment

*That's human hair.*

*Gently used.*

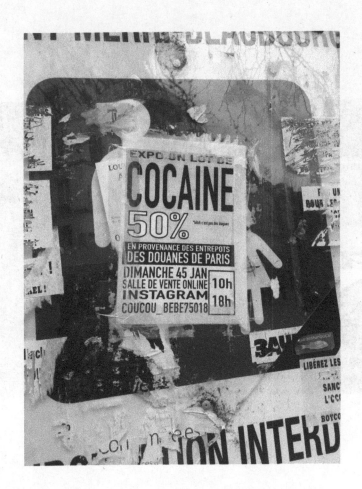

## Come Quick, Grandma's Been Taken

My mom was at the point in her disease where she had begun to lose her mind. This isn't a side effect of ALS, I think it was just something that happened due to her type A personality and pear shaped body type. Anyone would have lost their mind if they were dealing with what she was. In fact, I'm just surprised it didn't happen earlier.

About five months into her living in Provence, my mom began to have some difficulty breathing which then caused her to have a small panic attack. The panic attack was then exaggerated even further when the paramedics were not able to find the house. We heard the sirens circling the village since there wasn't anything to muffle the sound, but they couldn't seem to reach our house. After an hour, they found us. But, the power had gone out the night before as it did every night now, which reset the metal gate. Because it couldn't be opened automatically, the paramedics and firefighters had to jump the wall and maneuver their way through the bushes to get to the front door. They were finally able to strap my mom into a stretcher to take her to the hospital, but because of the comedy rule of three, the door was too narrow for the stretcher to fit through.

After some attempted maneuvers, they settled on plan B. She would just have to go out the window, like a fat person in a fire. This may have been the straw that broke the camel's back.

She ended up only living in Provence for six months or so, which is actually the average amount of time we lived in any house growing up as well. She had a habit of remodeling rentals and then acting surprised when the landlord asked us to leave before the lease was up. While Provence was beautiful, I think she started to realize that nothing beats convenience. Provence was culturally much more enlightened than anywhere in America, but it was lonely. David and I were only able to visit on the weekend because he had a job to go to and I was in my junior year of college at The American University of Paris. This was the year where I actually had a social life not only at the bar scene, but also at school. I was invested in my classes and study groups because these study groups usually ended up at a bar, but that's beside the point.

My mom had collected three pets while living there, hoping for some company, but the additional caring of the animals, lead to her caregivers quitting. It was completely understandable that they would quit, we were surprised they hadn't done it sooner. She had come to her senses and realized that it was probably time to go back to Paris. But, because she was beginning to develop a touch of cabin fever, she didn't explain this correctly to anyone involved. Any normal person would realize and understand that it's almost impossible to move cities with a day of notice. But, my mom left Provence the same day she decided to leave Provence. Apparently we would have known that she was moving home if we bothered to read her blog, where she had told everyone but us. I had not subscribed to her blog, because I didn't find it fun to look at photos of myself sleeping, but other people I guess did. She gathered a nice following, an extremely loyal following.

"Another care package is here!" I would yell out, "Looks like more handwritten love notes."

My mom was already dying, so she didn't mind giving out her address. She knew she couldn't be so unlucky that a deranged pervert would take time off from their job at the Foot Locker and come and strangle her to death. That just doesn't happen if you already have ALS.

I pretended to hate her blog, and I did on some level. I hated that she needed me to edit her photos and type the replies to the hundreds of comments she received. But, I did enjoy the perks. Once my mom wrote that she really wanted Chipotle, so the next week, a package arrived with hundreds of Chipotle gift cards. I sold them at school for slightly under the original value, netting myself a hefty profit.

These packages were becoming less frequent while she lived in Provence though, due to her address not being a place that mail went to, even Osama Bin Laden got mail. I could tell this bothered her, her blog was a huge part of her daily life, her connection to the world when she couldn't go out and live in it herself.

I had started to notice the frustration in her voice more and more, she became extremely impatient. If I didn't answer my phone, I would pay the consequences. She seemed to disregard my personal rule of no phone calls before 10 am nor after 10 pm. That was a pretty big window for conversation I thought. One morning, I received this voice message.

"Hi it's Mommy. Answer your phone you fucking brat. You're so spoiled. And stupid. Don't forget to take your birth control. Love you." If she didn't introduce herself I would have confused this message with the one Alec Baldwin had left his own daughter.

It was then followed by this email:

Hi my love,

I'm on the train to Paris right now and I need you

to meet me at the train station Gare du Nord at 3 so you can help take me to the palliative care center. Don't wear a dress or anything short, the train station has a lot of Algerians and I don't want you to get kidnapped. Maybe don't straighten your hair today. I love you butter.

I called her back while trying to get ready for school, straightening my hair anyways. The assailant would probably be turned off by the fact that I was not flexible enough to reach the back of my head and therefore could never straighten it. She had explained that she was moving back to Paris today but because she didn't have an apartment here anymore, the only way David agreed to facilitate it was if she stayed at the palliative care center until things were figured out. She did not explain her theory on the train station being an internationally known sex trading post.

Since she didn't technically have an emergency that warranted an actual hospital visit, she was going to stay at a medical facility, a palliative care center, where people went to be "put down". This was the place that people went to finish up their lives while having full-time medical care. It was a somber place, to say the least. But, it was also extremely hard to get into and it was pretty top notch. She had been checked into what they call "a garden suite" where she overlooked the rose gardens that overlooked the Seine. It was nicer than any of my apartments to date.

She had a little secret though, she wasn't going to end her life here, she just needed somewhere to stay while she house hunted. Her plan was going off without any of the normal roadblocks, she was really doing this. She arrived at the train station and immediately told me that I was looking paler than usual and then asked for me to get the dog from her seat. She had brought one of the three animals back with her. I honestly don't know where the other two went. She once gave away my chihuahua while I was in elementary school, so I knew what she was capable of and didn't care to ask.

Her entourage was taking their sweet time departing the train and gathering their belongings. I noticed my mom's blood slowly start to boil as steam came out of her ears. We share the same hatred for people who don't know how to chop chop. I don't understand why some people are slow. How is it possible to take ten minutes to heat up a pop tart that will only be in the toaster for one minute. It doesn't make sense. Slow people do not only burden themselves but everyone around them. They're always late and then, in turn, make me late, which I don't like. Slow people should have more consequences, I think that might solve the problem. There should be a rule: Every time someone takes longer than the needed amount of time to complete a task, whoever they're next to at that moment, is legally allowed to punch them in their face. Because said person is so slow, they probably wouldn't even have the reflexes to dodge it.

I tend to do all things rather quickly because I don't want to give people the option to wonder where I am out loud and possibly think I might be in the bathroom. "Maybe she's in the bathroom." No, stop that. Stop picturing me in the bathroom, that is disgusting. If I do ever go to the bathroom, I give an excuse, like I need to take a shower or I need to organize under the sink. This has worked very well thanks to my excellent timing and training my body. I'm prepared and willing to go to the Russian Olympics. I have had to take many unnecessary showers because of this method. I found out that it isn't fooling anyone if you just turn on the shower and then later leave the bathroom naked but dry. You have to actually get in the shower.

We arrived at the palliative care center and my mom gave the place a once over.

"Is this it?" She asked, "Is this really the best you guys could do?" She didn't hide her disdain for the decor of grey leather couches and Home Depot tile flooring.

"You don't like dead-girl-found-in-river grey?" I asked her

171

motioning to the paint on the walls.

"Let me show you to your suite, Madame." The nurse said surprisingly in English and pointed us to her ground floor room. It was large and had its own bathroom as well as a living room area near the window with a tv and pull out couch. But, it also kinda resembled a youth hostel in the red light district. I hung around for a few hours and then headed home to my charming 7th-floor walkup. This apartment was my least favorite because there was no wall separating the bathroom from the kitchen. My landlord had heard the word "open space concept" and ran with it before finishing the sentence.

The next morning I found myself visiting my mom in her new dorm room in Paris and not leaving until about three days later. Things weren't going exactly as planned and it seemed like this would be the end of her fight. She was losing motion in her head and had to wear an airplane neck pillow all hours of the day to keep her head propped up. It was no longer reserved for traveling. It was also becoming increasingly clear that she was about to emotionally give up on the fight as well. She was becoming angry and taking it out on anyone who would listen. I'm a weak a little bitch, so I took the insults she hurled at me to heart. But, I'm able to get over things quickly.

"I hope you get hit by a bus." She once yelled at me as I was leaving her hospital room to go to class.

"I hope you die before I get back!" I yelled back. The other residents in the hall were thankful they didn't speak English.

But, then 2 hours later, I would return from my class and be met with a big smile and mandatory hugs. I would show my mom a photo of a pair of boots I wanted and she would call me a slut for wanting over the knee boots. She wasn't aware that they were Stuart Weitzman and they would look great with my little black dress I had recently purchased with my grocery money.

Both my grandma and my aunt Heather decided to fly to Paris that week as well. My grandma doesn't like flying and it's fucking hilarious. On our first flight to Paris together, she clutched the arm rests the entire 11 hour flight and french kissed the ground when we landed. It was appropriate because we had in fact, just landed in France. This may have been the only time she was ever too nervous to eat.

"I'll eat when I land." She kept repeating every time food was offered to her. She then pulled out a bag of Puffy Cheetos as soon as we were taxiing in Charles de Gaulle.

Heather and my grandma flew in separately, where my Grandma would arrive a good six hours before her so she would have to make her way to the hospital alone. For a normal grandma, this might seem daunting, but for mine, it was easy. My grandfather, who was left at home had a harder time managing this and proceeded to purchase all his meals at CVS while she was away.

We received an email from him only 3 hours after my grandma's flight departed. It was a photo of Rosita's refried beans, still in the can, with a spoon. "Lunch," it said.

My grandma is not a typical grandma. Although she had just turned 70, she still looked 50. When we went to the DMV recently, they confused me as HER mother. Her favorite things in life are capri pants, Hillary Clinton and a Snickers bar. She would like you to know that she does not like Reese's though.

"I don't care for Reese's candy bars, I hate peanut butter." She announced, "But... If I had to have one, I would."

"Uhhhh in what world would you be forced to eat a Reese's?"

It seemed like an easy task for her to land at the airport and take a taxi to the exact address that she had written down. It's not like she was expected to fly the plane herself, she wasn't even expected to drive.

Her flight was supposed to land at noon, and by two, we still hadn't heard from her. Our first thought was that she crashed so we ruled that out by checking the status of her flight. It landed, on time. Then we imagined that she missed her flight entirely and was too embarrassed to tell anyone. We didn't really have a method to rule this one out, so it stayed on the back burner. Another two hours passed, and grandma was officially missing. But, we all weren't really that worried. She's gotten herself into worse situations and we had faith that she could find her way out of this one too. On her own. Also, no one knew how to report a missing person in France.

My Aunt Heather had now successfully arrived at the hospital and noticed that we were one man down.

"Uhh, where's mom?" Heather asked

"She's been sold into sex slavery." My mom replied. This was my grandfather's biggest fear about Europe. We were about to call him and tell him that his worst nightmare came true.

"Do they know she's not a virgin?" I asked and went back to zooming in on photos of Charlize Theron, "Do you think I look like her? Even a little bit?"

"No." The room replied.

We started to panic when the sun went down and still had no visual on the target. We started to imagine the image of my grandmother's naked dead body washing up in the Seine.

"She probably wouldn't be naked, she would be wearing that slutty nightgown she always wears." My aunt said. We all hated the nightgown. It was too short for anyone over the age of 13 and the lace had ripped over the 10 years she owned it, making it look "antique."

"Do you think we would see her float by from here?" I asked motioning towards the Seine view we had.

But, just as you speak of the Devil, in she came. The three of us whipped our heads around and hoped she hadn't over heard our conversation. But in all honesty, we probably would have had that conversation with or without her in the room. The best trait of my grandma was the fact that she was aware of how ridiculous she was and the enjoyment she got from watching us laugh at her.

"Well, well well." My mom said addressing my grandmother still standing in the door frame. "Where have you been?"

My grandma left the door frame and shuffled over to the couch, where she proceeded to take a Crunch bar out of her purse and begin to emotionally eat. "There was a strike at the airport, I couldn't leave."

"Uh, I was able to leave. Maybe they just weren't letting you leave." My aunt suggested.

"No no no. I couldn't get my luggage, they were protesting. I had to wait for them to stop the protest and get back to work before I was allowed to go to baggage claim." She said looking visually relieved now that she had some chocolate in her system.

"Do you know what they were protesting?"

"I don't know. I think it was about the baggage." She replied.

"They were protesting the baggage?" I asked confused.

She then described her journey to make her way over the hospital and all the trials and tribulations she experienced that day, her own personal Die Hard. Her phone had died because of the delay on the American side of the trip and her only charger was packed in her suitcase. When she arrived, she learned that she would not be getting her bag and that the entire team of airport baggage handlers had some beef with the bags (or so she thought). She decided that the best idea would be to patiently wait for the strike to be over to collect her belongings.

Over the next two weeks, my mom's decorum drastically declined. She had always been fond of verbal abuse, but usually, it was clever.

"Was there a half off sale? " She asked me the one time I wore a crop top. "Do you need to borrow money to buy the other half?"

Her abuse also began to spawn into multiple forms, one being Instagram. I have my own thoughts about Instagram and that I don't like it. It's really becoming a nightmare for someone like me who can't remember their password. My mom was much more into the digital era than I was. Her Instagram account boosted many more followers than I had or could afford to purchase. She posted regularly and would actually interact with her commenters. I do that too but only if I've had a cocktail in me. I'm much friendlier and not to mention funnier, when I've had a drink or three.

There was one nurse who wasn't all that attractive nor nice. She had a Lisa Rinna haircut and rosacea that was the color of the innards of a cherry pie. Her bedside manner was on par with a hyena.

The nurse's job was to come in check on my mom and adjust the bed, a turndown service. The other nurses usually stayed for a few minutes and refilled any empty water jugs and flower vases and generally went the extra mile. These patients were dying and they were there to make that process a little less miserable. But, this nurse didn't. She just wanted to get out of the room as soon as possible. Usually, this is something I can resonate with, as I usually wanted to leave my mom's room asap as well. But, she was getting paid for it, so there wasn't a viable reason as to why.

"Excuse me, may I have some more ice water." My mom would ask in her fake polite voice.

"No, we are out." She replied halfway out the door.

"You're out of water?" I asked surprised.

"Yes."

"What about ice? I can melt that, I'm in college, I know how." I said, proud of myself. Then forty-five minutes later she would bring a single ice cube as a compromise.

You couldn't help but not feel bad for her though. She never displayed any sympathy towards the patients and had one of those faces that was beyond resting bitch face. It was a full on frown, it was a resting cunt face. Why someone like her got into this business was beyond me. Maybe it was the family business? If it was, she must have been adopted.

What happened next is not entirely known and has now been taken to the grave by mom. She actually took a few secrets to the grave with her, most of which I don't have any interest in finding out.

"She punched me in the face!" My mother cried out one afternoon as I arrived.

"Who punched you?" I asked completely perplexed.

"The nurse who hates me, she punched me in my face."

"The nurse punched you in the face?" I asked thinking that I must have heard wrong.

"Yes, you have to call the police! You have to tell them that I'm paralyzed and I've been assaulted!" She said before turning her attention to the TV now that the commercial break was over.

"Sexually?" I asked.

I was not about to call the police. That was the last thing I wanted to do on my Friday afternoon off. I knew if I called the police with what was obviously a fake assault, I would be revoked of my French visa and forced to flee Europe before midterms started. Just kidding, I didn't have a visa.

"I think I got some potato chip in my eye. It really hurts. Can you look?" I asked changing the subject. I could feel a little bit of salt in my cornea. I had eaten potato chips on the metro ride over and had touched my eye before licking the salt off my fingers.

"Call the police!" She shouted as loud as she could.

"No!" I yelled back. "Do you want to order dinner or should I go grab something? How does Thai sound?"

The rest of the night went by without another mention of the "assault." She had told David after I left and he called me. He wasn't buying it either. She was trying to get out of the palliative care center and into an apartment and this seemed like the way to do it.

The next morning, I woke up at my apartment and proceeded with my morning ritual: roll over and read Daily Mail. It's not real news but interesting enough to reference in the phrase "Oh I read this article this morning..." and gain a few IQ points instantly. After Daily Mail, I looked at Instagram to see what everyone else is wearing that day and what activity I was left out of from the night before.

I scrolled past a posting from my mom that I usually ignored, but this one stood out. It was a photo of the nurse that had allegedly punched her with this caption:

"Last night I was abused by nurse Rose. I don't know her real name so I call her Rose because that is the color of her rosacea and the opposite of her personality. She has hit me in the stomach, punched me in the face and laughed at my suggestion that hemorrhoid cream might help her with two issues at once. She does not find me funny and I do not find her cute."

I chose to ignore this post and you would be surprised to know that this wasn't even one of her most offensive ones. I had grown a thick skin to her insults and sometimes forgot that other people hadn't. I simply brushed it off and assumed other people would think she was joking

By that afternoon, all hell had broken loose. Apparently someone in the hospital, followed my mom's Instagram account and told on her. She was now getting kicked out of the palliative care center for cyberbullying. A crime that, in my book, was not real.

"She has 24 hours before she is out on ze street." A woman explained to David and I.

"You can't do that, where is she supposed to go? To my house, where I live?" I asked terrified.

"Figure zit out." She said and stormed off.

David had begun scrolling through his phone, hoping an answer would lie right below his fingertips.

"Do you want to go figure this out over lunch?" I asked wanting lunch and David always chose a good restaurant. Something usually with tablecloths.

"No, I have to go to work. Go stay with your mom and don't let her use social media." He directed me, "You need to sleep here tonight. Look what happened when she was babysat by your grandmother and Heather."

I agreed that my mother would need a more forceful babysitter and I was known to crack the whip every now and then, for the right compensation of course. David let me order off of his UberEats account.

I snuggled up in the room for the night with my grandma, Heather, my mom and myself. It was like a Duggar family vacation, all crammed in one pull out couch, except of course, the Duggars never pulled out. I stared up and looked at the ceiling in agony. I couldn't sleep with all the medical equipment making metronome timed beeps. The only noise I was able to sleep to was Jimmy Kimmel reruns but ABC didn't reach France.

I eventually dozed off and woke up to the sweet serenade of my mother yelling at the nurse.

"You cannot kick me out, I am an American! This is unacceptable. Where am I supposed to go? Should I go to sleep on the subway? Huh? Should I come to your house?" She shouted.

"I'm sorry, she's an American," I said hoping the nurse would understand.

By that afternoon, my mom had crowdsourced her way out of the palliative care center. She would have liked me to say she left by choice, but we all know that that was not the case. The other patients had enough of her too. She had received multiple complaints from other patients that she and her TV was too loud and that she ordered too many deliveries.

"They're dying, wouldn't you think that they'd want a little

179

excitement?" My mom asked the room.

"I tried to tell the nurses that, but they're saying that's not the only reason we're not welcome here anymore." My aunt Heather replied.

"Are they still mad about the Instagram post. I'm not going to take it down, that's my second amendment right."

"Are you packing heat right now?" I chimed in.

"What are you talking about?" My mother had mixed up her amendments. "Gracie, give me my phone!" She said motioning her head towards the iPhone on the table.

It was always strange to have these arguments with her. While I knew she couldn't physically grab her own phone, I still couldn't disobey her and not hand it to her. I had been raised by fear alone. I never didn't do as I was told, so I never knew what the consequences were. The only time I ever disobeyed was when I was 8 and ran into a rapid river, despite not being allowed to. This was the only time I was spanked and I felt humiliated. I knew she couldn't spank me herself but her Filipino caregiver could. I don't know what would be more humiliating.

"You really should erase the post, they might let you stay here if you do. Maybe you should get a finsta." I suggested.

"No, make sure David doesn't erase my post, if I have to be the whistleblower, then I will. They will just have to kick me out." My mom said.

"OK, Snowden."

"Put my phone in between my legs so it's hidden."

"No way, your vagina is there."

"Just do it! Put on gloves."

"You can still get AIDS through gloves! I don't care what Princess Diana said. I've never had AIDS, so I think I know best."

"I'll buy you those Stuart Weitzman boots."

"Deal"

"You also need to help me pack up tomorrow and go to my new apartment. Remember, I already bought you."

She then had me wedge the phone in between her thighs so no one would dare grab it and erase her post. It really was the safest spot.

That afternoon I skipped through the street with my big purple Stuart Weitzman shopping bag. The boots were suede and wonderful. Later that night, I accidentally peed on them while trying not to touch a public toilet. I wore them the next afternoon when I went to help move my mom into her new apartment anyways, and the picture ended up getting removed from Instagram for violating their community guidelines.

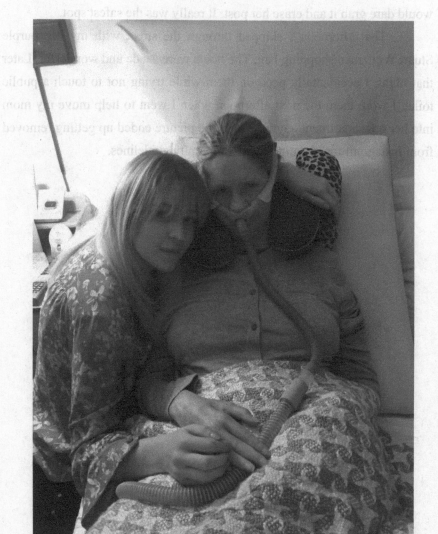

# Terms of Endearment

In August of 2016, my mom had decided that she had enough of France. She was tired of not seeing her friends and not having American cable. But her main complaint about France was that they didn't have Mexican food. The closest thing they had was a Chipotle and she wasn't about to give herself e.coli on top of ALS. She moved into the guest house behind the house that I grew up in on Miramar beach in Montecito. It was a small one bedroom cottage with a perfect little private yard and you could hear the waves breaking if you listened hard enough. It looked like the perfect place to learn how to make ceviche or kill yourself.

"Now that I live in California, I can't fly back for your graduation. Are you ok with that?" My mom asked.

"Yeah, I already gave away your ticket to someone else anyways." I kissed her on her forehead and went to steal her Moncler jacket.

"I might not be alive for your graduation either. Are you ok with that?"

"Yeah." I said sitting down inside her closet. I wasn't ok with that.

Even though I knew she was going to die, it was just starting to feel like she might live until forever. She had made it this far, why couldn't she just keep living until I died? When she asked for my permission to die, I gave her my permission. She had asked this many times, I always said something like "sure, whatever,", knowing she would change her mind later. She never was seriously considering dying. It was like getting bangs, she never actually got them, but she talked about them all the time.

Only once did I think she was serious. It was in 2014 in Paris. I was staying the night because I lost my apartment keys. She told me she was tired of living and I understood why. She was only leaving the apartment once a week because it was too difficult to fit her wheelchair in the elevator. This wasn't the way of life she wanted.

"Are you going to be alright without me?"

I finally told her the truth, "No I won't be alright! I'll never be alright if I have to live without my mom. I don't want to not have a mom! I'm too scared to do this alone, to do this life thing without you."

I now was sitting in her bed, laughing about using her death as an excuse to get out of completing my art history thesis. She told me that I was only allowed to be sad for a year and then I had to move on.

Her friend Hollye came over with paperwork about hospice and how she could legally complete assisted suicide. Lots of needles, too many needles.

"What if I just stop eating? And only take the drugs that Micheal Jackson used?" My mom asked logically.

"Well you could do that, but the drugs would have to be administered by you. If someone else puts the drugs in your feeding tube or mouth, they would be responsible for your death, like Micheal Jackson's doctor." Hollye replied.

Why was it so hard to kill yourself? My mom had looked into an assisted suicide program in Switzerland but you had to live with the nurses for a week before so they "could get to know you." My mom decided against this, as she didn't want her final week to be spent getting molested by Swiss nurses.

Hollye left the paperwork with my mom and let us think about the options together. In order for no one to go to jail for her murder, she would have to go the hospice route. It would be a longer process but it would be legal.

My mom looked at me sitting on the couch at the end of her bed, "Come here."

I climbed up into her bed, like I had done so many times before, and laid down next to her.

Up until the age of 10, I insisted on sleeping in her bed every night. She never minded until one time I wet the bed and ruined her Anichini sheets. Even after that, she still let me. I even demanded that I be allowed to take showers with her well after the age it was appropriate. I just wanted to be close to her. When I got to college, I decided that she was a loser and lost all interest in being her friend, let alone showering with her. But, I still called her from the girl's bathroom to tell her what I was going to eat for lunch. I still asked her to make me a chai latte (or ask her to ask her caregivers). I still wanted her to think I was the best thing that ever happened to her.

"I don't think I can keep doing this anymore." My mom said.

"Do what?" I asked curiously.

"Live."

"Ok."

I had gotten so used to talking about her death that I was almost desensitized by the whole thing. She would change her mind about this later, like she always did. She told me to hold her hand and I did.

"Can we take a selfie together?" She asked.

I took out my phone and held the camera in front of us, "Ugh, nevermind," She said in horror of what she looked like. She never really saw her face anymore. Her wheelchair was too short for the bathroom mirror. Her once slender face was now puffy from all the supplements she was on. Her blonde hair now had black roots down to her ears, she couldn't hold her head up long enough to get highlights anymore. She didn't look like my mom anymore, she just looked sick. I took a photo of our hands instead.

"I'm going to leave you little notes for you to open when I'm gone. Open one up every time you feel sad."

I nodded yes.

"You can't be sad though, because you know I'll still be here right?"

I nodded again.

"You just have to look for butterflies and ladybugs and peonies and I'll be there."

I nodded. I knew if I spoke word vomit would pour of my mouth, begging her not to die.

"Do you know how much I love you? I love you the most, more than anyone has ever loved anyone, I love you more than that actually. I love you more than I love myself. You were the best thing that has ever happened to me."

"I love you too." I murmured.

"I know you're pretending like this isn't hard. You don't have to be strong forever, I just don't want you to be sad. The love I have for you is so much more than most people ever get, I'm lucky to have had you this long."

I laid my head on her chest and tried my hardest to be strong one last time. Strong enough to convince her that I would be okay without her, even though I wouldn't be. I didn't have a choice though.

"I'm going to see you again, I promise." She reassured me. I didn't know if she was talking about in Heaven or Thanksgiving break.

Yolanda came into the room, it was time to leave for my flight. I didn't want to leave, I had a sinking feeling that this really was the last time I was going to see her. The other side of my mind convinced me that she wasn't going to really die. *Remember, she did this all the time.*

I stood up from the bed and wiped my eyes. Then wiped my mom's eyes. I laid my body across her body and hugged her as much as I could without hurting her.

"I love you Mommy" I said.

I walked to the doorway and she called back, "Wait, one more."

I reentered the room and hugged her again.

I held her hands as far as my arms could stretch before I had to let go. I stood at the doorway again and said, "I love you Mommy." I walked into the living room, I could hear my mom crying in the background.

I turned around once more and hugged her, this time tight. Do you remember that scene in Terms of Endearment when Debra Winger is telling her kids goodbye? This was a million times worse. My mom made me watch that movie with her a few years before we reenacted it. I bit the inside of my cheeks to try not to cry the entire time. It didn't work. I imagine my mom watching that movie when it came out, crying for an entirely different reason than she did when we watched it together.

I walked out of her house that day 3 hours later than intended. I couldn't let go, even though I was sure that nothing bad was going to happen. She wasn't actually going to die, I'll see her again, I kept repeating in my head. But this goodbye felt different.

Three years before, when I left for college, my mom cried and begged me to drop out. She ended up moving to Paris to be closer to me, I figured this goodbye would turn out like that. At least I hoped it would.

Yolanda drove me to LAX and held my hand until I boarded. I got on the plane feeling excited about my senior year. I called my mom to tell her I got a window seat.

The next day, I landed in Paris. I breathed in the stale air and blew out second hand smoke. I called an Uber on David's account and hauled my three suitcases into the van. I didn't have an apartment yet, but that wasn't an issue. I had booked a hotel in the 7th arrondissement for the time being. I had an appointment with the housing office at school later that week. Since I only had leftover birthday cash as my means for living, I booked the cheapest hotel I could find that was within walking distance from campus. The photos of the place didn't look all that bad, it looked clean enough. I figured I would be out painting the town red for most of my stay anyways.

When I pulled up to the hotel, no one came out to help. There was a small door that was next to the supermarket that said "Hotel" in gold lettering. The window had bars on it. I arrived at the hotel expected to be greeted, but I guess I had forgotten that I flown to Iraq by accident. There was bulletproof security entrance after the front door that I pushed my way through with my bags. Just from looking at me you could tell that I was not able to haul these bags by myself. I had only eaten one meal on the flight and I was practically wasting away. But, given no choice, I rolled up to the check in desk and was handed my key. The man checking me in had one eye and didn't bother putting a patch over the empty socket. He handed me my key and pointed me to the elevator.

The room was so small that I had to vertically stack my suitcases against a wall. I called my mom to tell her how small my hotel was but she didn't answer.

After taking a whores bath as not to rinse away my spray tan, I decided I was going to go spend all the money I had. It was 90 degrees in Paris that day, but that wasn't going to stop me from wearing the outfit I planned, a black skirt with a white thick cotton turtleneck sweater. I thought since it was white, it worked as a 'summer sweater.' I went directly to Sandro to purchase my new fall wardrobe. While I was busy buying boots I couldn't afford, my spray tan was busy dripping down my back. But just in patches, where I was sweating the most. I boarded the subway with my giant shoe box and onset vitiligo surrounded by French people who were clearly whispering about me. I took my seat and tried to pat my spray tan dry with the tissue paper from the bags. It wasn't working, the paper was just sticking to my legs now. I got off the metro and walked the remaining few blocks. I stopped along the way to grab takeout at a Chinese restaurant. This wasn't how I was expecting my first night in Paris to go.

The takeout wasn't very good and I couldn't figure out how to connect to wifi, so I just went to sleep.

I've heard stories about people waking up in the middle of the night with an overwhelming sense that something is wrong, and then they later find out that someone they loved died or Trump was elected, but I didn't believe they were true. They were things people would tell you when trying to convince you that they had a sixth sense.

That night at 1am, I woke up. I woke up quick and suddenly, as if someone just sat on my chest. I looked around the dark room with the sense that someone was watching me. That was impossible though, the room had a maximum occupancy limit of one. I tried to go back to sleep but couldn't. Then my phone rang.

It was a facetime request from my Aunt Heather. I didn't understand why she would be facetiming me, we never facetimed. I silenced the ring and stared at my phone waiting for the call to end. But, without even thinking, I answered before it went to voicemail.

Her face appeared on the screen. She was outside and I could see the palm trees and blue sky behind her. She was crying.

"Gracie, I have to tell you something." She paused and looked away from the camera. "Your mom passed away."

The room started to spin and a knot welled up in my throat. The sign that an outpouring of tears was imminent. I laid back down only being able to whisper the words "no" inbetween dry heaves.

David got on the phone and tried to console me. It didn't work. I was alone in a shitty hotel room receiving the worst news of my life via a facetime call. This wasn't the way it was supposed to happen.

My mom had very specific plans on how I would find out she died. She told me she didn't want me to be there when she died because her body wouldn't let her die if she knew I was there. She planned to have someone deliver the news to me in person, either David or my friend Eliot. She didn't want me to be alone when my whole world changed. She was polite like that.

David talked to me for 30 minutes, I didn't say anything, I just cried and tried to angle the phone so he couldn't see me. The call ended with him forwarding me a boarding pass for a flight home tomorrow.

I didn't know what I was supposed to do when the call ended. Was I just supposed to go back to sleep? Take a shower? In none of the movies did someone receive news like this alone, I wasn't sure how to act. I curled up into fetal position and held my knees until they went numb.

I stayed in the same spot on the bed and tried to stop crying but I couldn't. My face began to swell and for the first time, I didn't care what I looked like. I had run this scene over in my head many times before, trying to picture what this moment would feel like. It felt like I imagined it would, only infinity times worse. I was in shock, even though I was expecting this news for the past six years.

I called Eliot but they didn't answer. Then I called my dad to tell him the news. Normally, I love breaking bad news to people. I called everyone I knew when Amy Winehouse died trying to be the first person to tell them that she overdosed. I dreaded this call though, and I didn't have to make it, but something inside of me dialed the number for me.

"Oh oh, oh no." He said when I told him.

I called my other dad, John, after and repeated the process. He stayed on the phone with me for a while and told me the story of when they got married. They had only met each other a week before. I smiled as he told me about meeting me for the first time.

The phone call ended and it was now 3 am. I went to the window and lit a cigarette, hoping the alarm wouldn't sound, it didn't. I looked out to the Parisian street and wondered, "What now?"

Eliot called me back, "Graaaccie where are you?" I could hear the barman yelling last call in the background.

"My mom died." I said slowly.

Eliot arrived at my hotel 20 minutes later. I tried to act like I wasn't sad because I didn't want to make them sad too. We ordered mozzarella sticks and chicken wings and two bottles of wine and a six pack of Heineken and charged it to their dad's amex. We searched the entire hotel room for a corkscrew and couldn't find anything. We finally had something so I could distract myself. We attempted to open the bottle any way Youtube recommend, but nothing seemed to work.

"I'll go to the front desk," Eliot offered, "They have to have one."

After a few minutes, Eliot returned holding one of the bottles of wine and two gin and tonics. Apparently this hotel did not have a corkscrew, because someone had stolen it earlier that day and had nothing that could be of any help. They had called a parlay with the bartender and had managed to barter with him a trade, one bottle of wine for two gin and tonics. It worked. We sat in that hotel room and drank until I left for the airport. I left my suitcases with Eliot and packed my purse with the essentials: a hair straightener, tanning mousse and tic tacs. I could just buy new things when I got home, I couldn't pack right now.

I was waiting to board my flight back to LAX, then it was delayed, delayed a little more and then a few more hours. A delayed flight makes me panic and it is also when I would prefer to take my Mensa exam, as I am the smartest I ever can be at this exact moment. I called the airline to figure out what the fuck is going on. The woman on the other end told me this flight might be canceled, and that was good enough a reason for me to get off it. I called David and he told me to rush over to the Air France counter and book the next flight with them. Once there, I managed to score one of the last seats on a flight leaving in 30 minutes. But, my teen debit card has a daily spending allowance of $25, and I already had spent that on magazines at the gate. David called and tried to talk them into charging his card over the phone, because usually when David talks to someone, they kinda just do what he says. He managed to buy the ticket but I only had 25 minutes until the boarding gate closed. It was my own personal Mission Impossible, also I am roughly the size of Tom Cruise.

I ran towards security and made it to the gate, and to my sweet delight, David had booked me in Premium, so things were looking up. I sat down in my seat and passed out before I received my complimentary glass of champagne. I had been up for about 48 hours at this point and hadn't even figured out what time zone I was in. When I woke up three hours later, I assumed we would be ready for our first meal. My favorite food is airplane food. I love the little bread rolls and the dessert tart and the endless Coca-Cola. But, we had not left the tarmac and were now instructed to deplane the aircraft. Once off, we were told we would be switching planes. I followed the crowds and got onto a shuttle that was supposed to take us to the new plane and we would be on our way. False alarm. The shuttle was stopped and we were informed that this flight was now cancelled. My brain started going into overdrive and then my inner genius (Don't you wish I said inner goddess like in Fifty Shades of Grey?) emerged again. I called those motherfuckers at Air France, but even with all my rage, I had been taught that you catch more bees with honey, so I calmly spoke to the agent to arrange my next steps. Sike, I fucking cried. I cried so hard to the customer service agent.

"Linda, I just really need to get home," I snuck in between sobs.

"Everything is falling apart and I don't have a change of clothes and I'm so tired and so sad and please help me." I begged.

"Well, there's one flight leaving tomorrow and there's a few seats left on that flight. Would you like me to transfer you onto this flight." She said into I presumed was her wireless headset.

"Yes! Please! Can I also have an aisle seat?"

"I'm not sure yet ma'am, I'll need some information first."

After I was booked on the new flight, I found my way to the airport hotel and invited my friend Maggie to come stay with me for the night. I told her it was very luxurious and she was on her way. That was a lie, the hotel had the charm of a halfway house. We had dinner at the world's worst buffet that night and then retreated back to our suite. It was a ground floor freeway view bunk bed superior. As I was checking in for my flight online, I noticed that I had been booked in business class, and right then and there I knew my mom was with me. She understood me.

The next morning, I got dressed back into the only outfit I had with me, stone wash jeans that I had been suckered into buying at Sandro and my mom's white t-shirt. I boarded the shuttle bus back to the airport and checked into the lounge. I didn't have an appetite but forced myself to eat the scrambled eggs because they were free.

I boarded the flight and immediately unpacked the complementary pouch filled with chapstick and earplugs. I set aside the airplane socks they gave me to save for my mom. They were her favorite. I caught my mistake and put them on my feet instead.

Then out of all the people that could have sat down next to me, all the strangers in the world, someone I knew was booked beside me instead. My friend Nina. I hadn't seen her in over a year. We had a few classes together at college and went to London together for a birthday party once. Her mom and my mom were friends even. Nina's family owned a hotspot restaurant in L.A. that my mom be been frequenting since she was a teenager. If the free upgrade wasn't enough to show me my mom was with me, I now really was convinced.

"Oh my god, how weird is this? What are you going to L.A. for?" She asked as she set up her area.

"So crazy! School doesn't start for another week so I'm just flying home for the last week of summer. I had to come out early to get an apartment," I lied.

I didn't want to bother her with my news that my mom died. I just wanted to pretend like it didn't happen, at least for another ten hours. And so I did. I made up lie after lie as we chatted.

"How's your mom?" She asked.

"She's good, she's in Santa Barbara right now." Technically, that was true.

I lied some more as our meals arrived (with real cutlery!). There were two weird beige circular patties on a plate. They felt squishy when I pushed my fork into them. Nina cut one in half and so did I. I chewed and chewed but it just felt like it was bouncing around in my mouth like a 25 cent bouncy ball. Surprisingly delicious though! I later learned this was a scallop.

There was a pre-funeral planned at Miramar beach for this afternoon. Because of my flight delay, I would be arriving right as it started.

David picked me up from the airport and we laughed the entire drive up to Santa Barbara. We laughed that he had better blonde hair than me. We laughed that I didn't know what a scallop was. We laughed as we drove through Taco Bell. Then we got off the freeway exit and I got nauseous.

"I'm just going to stay up here for a minute." I told David as he walked down to the group of people waiting in the sand.

All of my mom's favorite people were down at the beach sharing memories of her and eating snacks. I knew the moment I walked down there, it would be real. I would be hit with condolences and offers if I "need anything, ever, don't hesitate to call."

I was now standing at the top of stairs leading down to the beach, dry heaving. This was the beach I grew up at. On Sunday mornings my mom gave me a choice, either go to a church service or go for a walk on the beach. I always choose the walk on the beach. We would walk until we were tired and talk until we ran out of words. This was so much more godly than service. After she got sick, she was given a beach wheelchair so we could continue this. Sadly we didn't go on many of these walks anymore. Mainly because the beach wheelchair was huge and looked like a ride at Chuck-e-Cheese.

I took an Ativan out of my purse and swallowed it dry, collected myself, and descended to the first of my mom's many memorials.

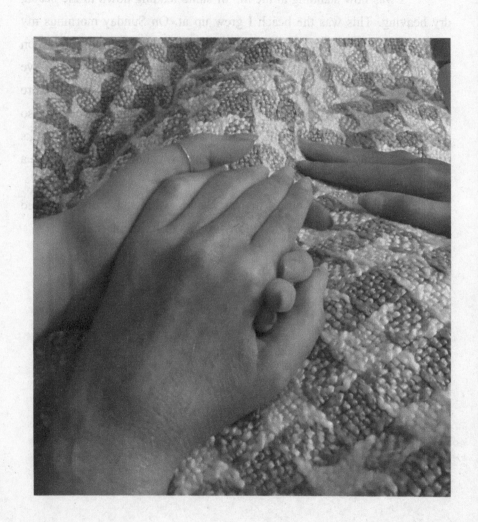

## The Sign

I would like to formally state that I am not a good person. I constantly judge other people based on their haircuts, I eat in bed and generally I dislike anyone from the Southwest. I was especially horrendous in the period after my mom's death and before her memorial. There were 2 months in between her passing and her formal memorial service, which is not normal. But, there was nothing normal about my mom so this was fitting. I had flown back to Paris to continue my final year at college during this in-between period.

I lived in my own studio apartment that had seven flights of stairs to get to it. So, I hardly left. I would order takeout and have the delivery guy climb my stairs and then close the door before he could request his tip. It's not like I had a tip to give him, I spent my weekly allowance already on said takeout. I would then take my tikka masala and eat it out of the metal container in bed while smoking a cigarette. The curry would make me tired and I would fall asleep before I had a chance to crack a window. When I woke up the next day, my apartment smelled like the inside of Hulk Hogan's gym bag.

Even if I didn't fall asleep immediately after eating an entire buffet of takeout, I hardly opened my windows. I didn't like the feeling of the fresh breeze. I could hear children in the street laughing and wished they would get hit by a bus. The one night I did leave my window open I woke up and there was someone else's cat in my bed. My windows only had sheer panel curtains that didn't do anything other than let anyone know I had visited IKEA recently. I used to hang my comforter over my window and secure it with hair bands. I then put on a coat and went to sleep without a blanket. My heater wasn't working either. It had recently caught on fire and I had to put it out with a glass of Sprite. I never told my landlord about this so it never got fixed.

The entire month of September was spent repeating this process. I didn't go to class either. I just emailed all my professors that my mom had died and got out of all responsibility. It's the least they could do. Instead of doing the homework assignments they emailed me, I would handwrite out calendars and count down the days I had left until graduation. I didn't know where I was going next, I didn't have a home to go back to anyways. I just didn't want to be here anymore. Paris was my mom's city, not mine.

I got it in my head one day that I should drop out of college. It seemed like the most logical and dramatic choice for me. I didn't think it mattered whether or not I had a college education, we were all going to die anyway. I ran into Eliot at the admissions office and told them my plan.

"Why don't you go to therapy instead?" Eliot suggested.

I got the therapist's information and said I would make an appointment. I never went. I told Eliot that I enjoyed my session with him and he suggested that I follow my gut and drop out.

"The therapist is a woman though." I was caught.

I called David and he told me I was acting like a douchebag and that he would not let me drop out of school. David has always been one of the only people I actually listened to. Instead of dropping out, I decided I would start working out and only eating one meal a day. I got down to 100 pounds before anyone said anything.

"You look so good." A girl said as I chewed on my cuticles.

"Thanks, I stopped eating."

I believe this period of time was the only time I was truly sad. Normally, stress and sadness cause me to overeat, a time-honored O'Connell tradition. If I got a bad grade or got caught gossiping, I would take myself out to lunch and order as if I had a baby on the way. But, this time I had lost my appetite and it didn't feel like it would be coming back anytime soon. No amount of macaroons would fix this hole inside me. I would force myself to eat a bowl of chili every other day when I started feeling faint.

It was now October and the memorial service was coming up soon. David had scheduled the service for October 16th. The entire time leading up to it, I felt like I was in limbo and my mom must have felt that too. I tried to picture what she was doing in heaven but I couldn't shake the feeling that she wasn't actually gone. I sometimes would convince myself that she was just away on a business trip and this was all a misunderstanding.

I sat on my floor and tried to pack but felt too weak. My hands could barely lift up the wool Prada dress I had my mom pre-approve for the service. I dropped it back onto the floor and laid down instead. I stared up at the ceiling and took note of how ugly the light fixture was. It was a round pink paper lantern over a lightbulb. Every day looked like a quinceanera. I started to cry.

I'm a firm believer that once you start crying, it's important to get everything out. Otherwise, you'll find yourself finishing said cry in a gas station bathroom. I turned on the song that always made me think of my mom, Jewel's "You Were Meant For Me." It's a breakup song but that never phased me.

"I got my eggs, I got my pancakes too." I shouted through my tears singing along, "I got my maple syrup, everything but you."

I paused to wipe my nose on my sleeve.

"Dreams last so long, even after you're gone. I know, that you love me."

My mom used to listen to this song as she did chores around the house. She had downloaded it from Limewire so half through Bill Clinton would interrupt, "I did not have sexual relations with that woman," and then the song would keep playing.

I tried to light a cigarette but my hands were too wet from tears and snot to hold the lighter properly. I felt completely alone in this dumb apartment. I hated the dumb floors and the dumb wallpaper. I hated the dumb one burner stove and the dumb bathroom that didn't have a door. The sun had set an hour ago and the apartment was now dark. I didn't get up to turn the lights on for another 30 minutes because the dark felt right.

After crying for two hours my mind started to wander, I forgot what I was crying about in the first place. I thought about what I would be for Halloween and wondered if it was too soon to dress up like Susan Atkins. I pictured myself gently creating an eyeshadow mustache to really get into character. The tears began to dry and my face began to swell. I stood up and turned the lights on finally but went right back to my spot on the floor. I thought about the time my mom caught me reading Helter Skelter under my covers and remembered why I was sad again.

I then did something that I never did before. I said a prayer that wasn't forced upon me at a dinner table or Easter service. I prayed for a sign. For a sign that my mom was still here with me. I hadn't seen anything since she died and was beginning to lose faith and that death really was the end.

"If you're there move my stupid paper lantern! You have to do this to show me you're here and you're listening to me. You have to. You can't leave me alone!"

Then, the lamp swayed. I swear to God, the lamp swayed like a breeze had just rolled in. But there hadn't been any fresh airflow in that room for two weeks. I sat up quickly as fast as I could with my new situp earned abs. I stared at the lantern moving back and forth, it wasn't slowing down. I rubbed my eyes worried I was hallucinating. That the chili I ate was drugged. But, it was real. I had my sign. I fell asleep that night still watching my lantern sway.

One day later, I was back in California. David picked me up from the airport and I felt remarkably better. I had gotten the sign I was looking for and everything all of a sudden was coming up rainbows. I ate a meal at the airport and even washed my hair in the morning.

"I didn't pack anything to wear to the funeral, " I said as we were getting on the 405. "Can we go to Amber's really quick so I can grab some clothing?"

I realized I had forgotten to pack the Prada dress and instead only packed Lululemon leggings. They were black but even I knew they were inappropriate to wear to a funeral.

Amber owned a clothing company called Flynn Skye and she had told me to stop by and grab some clothes when I landed. She knew it was important that I didn't look like the mess I had become, at least for one day.

Amber handed me a stack of black bodysuits. "Wear one of these with some cool black pants and heels."

"Is this one too slutty?" I asked holding up a deep V-neck long sleeve bodysuit.

"No, it's perfect!" She said and added some pants to my loot pile.

The high of getting free clothes made me forget about the reason I was receiving the clothes. I had to attend my mom's funeral in two days. I have low moments where all I can think about is my mom and how unfair the whole deal was. Then I have moments where I forget about her death completely until I remember and feel bad for forgetting. It's a vicious cycle. I will sometimes forget that she died. This usually happens when I'm experiencing a real high in my life. I'll be so excited and can only think about the present. Then I'll immediately think of my mom and want to tell her, forgetting that she died entirely.

David and I arrived in Santa Barbara later that night. The memorial was in two days and we had some planning to do. My mom had left us very specific instructions for the day.

Four months ago I was laying next to my mom in bed, writing out her funeral requests. She wanted everyone to dress in all black. She wanted white lilies placed around the altar for the church service. Try to get security to work the door. At the reception after, it was to be catered by the Pierre Lafond bakery. She even specified which tea sandwiches to get, chicken and tuna salad, absolutely no ham. The house cocktail should be a lemon drop martini. Gifts encouraged.

The night before the service, my dad flew into town and took me a Van Morrison concert. I only knew "Brown Eyed Girl" but it was a welcomed distraction. He dropped me off and I found myself wide awake in bed, staring at the ceiling again. I was staying at my friend Madison's house where the ceiling was much nicer than my apartment's ceiling.

7 am came and I was already awake when my alarm rang. I put on my Amber approved outfit and tried to apply a winged eye. As always, one turned out much better than the other. I put on sunglasses instead. The service wasn't until 3 pm that day, so I wore Uggs instead of heels. I knew my mom wouldn't be happy with that choice but she wasn't here to stop me anymore.

My mom hated Uggs and refused to purchase me any, no matter how many times I begged. I began saving up the coins I found in the couch cushions and money I took from the bottom of her purse, so one day I could buy my feet the treat they deserve. I finally saved up $100 and went to my mom's room to request a ride to Nordstroms. I found her organizing her sweater collection while wearing David's Uggs. I got to save my $100 and my mom bought me the Uggs as blackmail.

David and I pulled up to Pierre Lafond to get the very important sandwiches. I had spent every morning here when I was in elementary school. My mom would buy a chai latte and I would pick out the biggest chocolate croissant from the case. The bakery looked the same but felt like walking into an alternate universe, a universe that my mom didn't exist in. I wanted to scream at the customers for acting like everything was normal.

I went to go order the sandwiches. I could hear my mom over my shoulder, *make sure to request fresh lettuce on the sandwiches.*

"Please make sure the lettuce is fresh and crunchy for each sandwich," I said to the man behind the deli. I was now acting as my mom's earthly vessel for her anal retentiveness.

We went to go drop off the sandwiches at the reception location. *Go make sure they use Tito's vodka in the martinis.* Again I acted as she wished. Maybe I was possessed? I felt her presence all the way until the service, making sure everything was up to her standards.

David and I arrived at 2 pm on Miramar beach. He went around to the trunk of the car and pulled out a blue and white chinoiserie pot filled with my mom's ashes. She had requested that we spread half her ashes at the beach and the other half at the Palais Royal in Paris. It had been arranged that my mom's favorite 20 people meet us at the beach an hour before the service began. This was to be the VIP section.

People began to arrive and I managed to keep it together until I saw Jenny. Jenny was my mom's bestest friend in the whole wide world. She was the coolest and funniest person alive and always had the best hair products. I would look forward to showering at her house so I could use her fancy conditioner. I sometimes wished she was my mom. As soon as

Jenny walked down to the beach I started to cry. She loved my mom as much as I did, maybe even a little bit more.

We all walked along the beach, unable to pick a spot. We just kept walking, looking for any reason not to choose a certain spot. Too crowded. Ugly beach house. Too many rocks. I was the main culprit for 86'ing a spot. I knew that the moment we choose a place, it was official, she was gone. We were choosing her final resting place and I wanted to put it off even if it was just for another 15 seconds. But, when we reached the spot, about half a mile down the beach, I knew it was the place.

The old Miramar beachfront hotel was in the process of being torn down for a new hotel. The Miramar Inn had been abandoned for the past 15 years. My mom and I used to ride our bikes over to the spot where the chain link fence had a hole in it and sneak in. We would walk up to the windows of the cottages and peak in. She would tell me about her plan to remodel the hotel while trying to open the door to get a better look inside. The hotel had been bought and sold a handful of times over the years. No one was able to accomplish anything other than demolishing a few of the buildings before permit restrictions kicked in and they backed out. Now, in 2016, there was finally a plan in action to turn this abandoned beachfront property into a 5-star resort. This spot in the sand was prime for watching the remodel.

"What about here? Mom can watch the hotel being built from here." I said to David.

"Oh, it's perfect." He replied and stopped the group from walking any further.

We gathered around in a large circle and David said a few words. I couldn't speak. I just held Yolanda's hand and pinched my leg to hold off the tears. David reached into the vase and pulled out a handful of ashes. He tossed them into the sand but the wind blew them back onto our feet. David wiped the ashes off his hands onto his pants, leaving small traces of what remained of my mom. She made it clear that she didn't want her ashes to be in the ocean, just near it. Even in death, she was afraid she was going to drown.

It was clear how much these people loved my mom. No one else was able to speak over their tears. Yolanda jumped to the center of the group and began arranging the flowers into a heart shape.

"We have to make it pretty for Ellie," Yolanda said looking for rocks to stack in the center of the heart.

We heard splashing in the ocean and looked to expect a kid body surfing in the waves. Instead, it was a group of five dolphins swimming only a few feet away from shore. My mom was coming through with the signs like she promised. We all started to shout in amazement. There was no way this was a coincidence. My tears of sadness turned into tears of happiness. To an outsider, they look exactly the same. But, when I'm sad I feel the tears welling up in the throat, when I'm happy, it feels like they're going to come out of my smile.

It was time to walk back over to the church for the service. The church was next door to my childhood home. It was the only house I ever consider to be my home. There were two cars parked in the driveway and I thought about how lucky that family was to be living there. It was a happy house. I pictured my mom haunting it later.

When we turned the corner to the front of the Church, there was a crowd of 200. My mom was right, we probably should have hired security. Every person there had a memory of my mom and couldn't wait to share it with me. I couldn't remember most of their names.

David and I sat in the front row with Jenny, Yolanda and I can't remember who else. The speakers for the event kept changing in the moments leading up to the service.

"I can't do it, I won't be able to get through it."

The service began and I fixated my eyes on the framed photo of my mom at the altar. She was wearing a long blue and white dress and standing in what would be her other final resting place, the Palais Royal. How morbid. I had seen this photo hundreds of times, she had even chosen this as her memorial photo herself. But, this time it looked different. In fact, every photo of my mom looks different after she died. I stare at her face every time I see a photo of her and try to remember what she sounds like. It's hard to remember what someone's voice sounds like even when they are alive. I squinted my eyes and tried to zoom in on the photo from across the room. I couldn't articulate my thoughts in my own head, other than saying to myself, *that was my mom.*

The music began to play and the first row was lead out. I held David's hand for the first time in my life as we walked out. I kept my head low, trying not to look at every one. When we reached the end of the pews, I looked up and saw that people were standing all around the back of the church. The seats had filled up completely. My mom sold out the show, of course, she did.

To be competitive, which my mom would have wanted me to be, I would say she won the funeral. The service was beautiful. I stood with David at the entrance to the church and pretended to recognize all the people that came up to hug me. Everyone was wearing sunglasses and hats so that wasn't helping.

Everyone began to file out and head over to the Nesbitt's for the reception and to get their hands on a much needed lemon drop. I walked back over to the beach and said goodbye. I felt strange leaving her there but I didn't have a choice. As much as I wanted to go sift through the sand, gather her ashes and eat them, I knew that it was time to focus on making myself the person she wanted me to be. She wanted me to graduate college, she wanted to be there for it. Her original "death plan" was to survive until my graduation, even though I told her she wasn't invited. In the end, she didn't make it that long, but I wasn't allowed to take that as a sign that I didn't have to finish. She would rise from the dead and spank me if I did that. I also needed to learn French finally.

When I arrived at the reception, I was greeted by a fleet of Range Rovers and smiles. Everyone seemed to have forgotten that we were just at a funeral and I couldn't be happier about it. People always say that when they die they don't want their funeral to be sad, they want it to be a celebration of their life. I used to think that was bologna until my mom's. People were gathered around tables sharing stories about my mom.

My mom's friend Melinda told me about the time she and my mom got out of speeding ticket. Melinda was 13 and my mom was 15. They had taken my grandpa's new Porsche out for a test run around Malibu. Melinda was driving when they heard the police's sirens behind them.

"Quick switch seats with me, you're older!" Melinda shouted to my mom. Neither had driver's licenses.

After they swapped spots, the cop came over to the driver's side door and asked for my mom's license and registration.

"I forgot it at home, there was an emergency and had to rush out." My mom said trying to look like a damsel in distress.

"Well, what's the emergency miss?" He asked peeking inside the car.

"She had a botched abortion!!" My mom shouted and pointed to Melinda.

Melinda grabbed her crotch and began to scream in pain. The cop, clearly uncomfortable by the fake back alley underage abortion, let them go. They high fived as they drove away like Thelma and Louise.

Over the years, I heard more and more of these stories. My mom must have thought I was such a dork for crying when I got a parking ticket.

The sun was setting and I didn't want the day to end. The day I dreaded to arrive was becoming a rather joyous occasion. I hadn't cried in hours. I knew that this would be the last time I would see all these people together. It would also be the last time I was the center of attention until my birthday. This would also be the last event that was thrown in honor of my mom, the last time anyone would celebrate her. I still celebrate her birthday every year but I know not everyone does the same.

Your funeral really is the last time people focus on you. After that, it's just memories that pop up out of the blue to remind you. You no longer have anyone's 100% attention. Even when I sit and think about my mom, something else is always on my mind.

David and I were on a flight back to Paris the next morning together. I grabbed a magazine from the pile I purchased at the airport. UsWeekly was running a Princess Diana tribute in honor of the anniversary of her death. I reached for my phone to text my mom that she and Di almost shared a death date, and then I realized.

My mom's shrine to me.

# Therapy Shmerapy

I had just moved to LA and purchased my first car. I had cars before, but this was the first one that I picked out and I was paying for. When I turned sixteen, my dad gave me his old car. A three-tone red Volvo station wagon. The car looked like it had been purchased in pieces. The hood was a dull brown-red, like old blood. The middle section was bright cherry red and the trunk was the same cherry red but matte. I had gotten into a fight with him when I asked if I could use my own money to paint the car black. He argued that I should be saving that money for college and I argued that he didn't understand the backlash of driving a car that looked like a used maxi pad.

Three months after this fight, I got into a car crash that totaled my car. I was driving on the 101 in Santa Barbara when I looked in the rearview mirror and saw a car barreling towards me.

*Wow, they're going really fast.* I thought. *I hope they don't hit me.*

The car hit mine going 70mph and pushed my car off the freeway and into a tree. Everyone was somehow completely unscathed and I collected the insurance payout. Since the car was from the 1800's, the payout wasn't enough to buy a new car. I ended up just driving David's old Saab for the remaining months in Santa Barbara before moving to Paris. This car was in the same condition as Heidi Klum's legs, perfect. There was even cable TV in it.

When I moved back to LA in 2017, the very first day I went to Volkswagon and got a brand new black Tiguan SUV. The high of owning my first car faded away when I was notified about my first upcoming payment.

The car had something installed in it called "Carplay", where my phone, when plugged in, would sync up and everything was voice controlled. I could say, "Siri, Play 'Rich Girl' by Hall and Oates" and the car would obey. It would even read my texts out loud and then I could reply by speaking my response. It felt like driving a spaceship and it was more than my simple brain could handle. Only a few months earlier had I learned how to use the internet.

By September, I had a job, a car and an apartment. I was almost an adult, all I needed was a 401K. I planned on looking into getting one of those as soon as I learned what it was. I was working for my mom's friend Amber's clothing line, Flynn Skye. I had interned for her a few times over the years and we both agreed that I was the employee of the month. When I graduated, she offered me a full time job and I was over the moon excited to start working for her. Amber has created the ultimate L.A. cool girl brand because she is one of those cool girls. I would have accepted the position even if I was only paid in free lunch and some tops. On top of all the perks of having a cool boss, the work schedule was pretty relaxed. We were allowed to show up sometime between 9 am and 10 am, but because I am anal, I was there at 9am every morning. We would leave when our work was done, usually always before 5pm.

I was driving home from work one afternoon in my cute new car listening to the sweet sound of Bruce Springsteen and trying to match his vocals on "I'm On Fire" unsuccessfully, when the British woman who lives inside my phone, shouted over the speakers, "One new message from 'Grandma New'."

It wasn't from my new grandma, it was from my regular grandma. She has had so many phone numbers over the years that I have to specify which is which. Right now I have five numbers for her.

I shouted back, "Read the message!"

"Grandma New says, 'Dennis is dead.' Would you like to reply?"

My heart fell into my butt. I reached to turn down the volume. I was at a traffic light on the corner of Robertson and Burton, so I knew I would be stuck here for a while. My hands began to white knuckle the steering wheel more than they normally do. I wanted out. I wanted out of this moment. I didn't want to be in this car anymore. I was exactly two blocks from my apartment, I could leave my car right here, walk home and the light still wouldn't have changed.

Dennis was my uncle. He was married to my aunt Heather and was the father of my two cousins, Jack and Cody. He and Heather had gotten divorced back in 2003. He then moved into my grandparent's house and lived with them for seven years. When my grandparents would move houses, they would always make sure that there was a room for Dennis and a place to park his van.

Dennis is from the very musical family, the Dragons. His father was the conductor Carmen Dragon, his mother was an opera singer and his brother was the Captain of Captain and Tennille. Dennis had formed his own music group called Surf Punks back in the 80's in Malibu. You may know them from their hits, "No Fat Chicks," and "Too Big For Her Top." He and my aunt got married in the 90's in the ultimate 90's fantasy wedding. My aunt Heather was 24 at the time but looked like the sweetest child bride in the west. Her wedding dress sleeves were bigger than her head and Dennis wore his board shorts. He was also only a year younger than my grandpa, which explains why they got along so well and remained roommates even after the marriage was over.

The light finally changed and I was able to park on the same block as my apartment, something that was rare because I was in West Hollywood and without a reserved parking spot. I left my Tupperware container in the car and didn't bother to retrieve it. This time I blamed it on the tragedy that had just happened, the other days I blamed it on having a wedgie. Once inside, I called my grandma for more information than her beautifully written text had given me.

Dennis had commited suicide. At the time, he was living up at his house/recording studio in Oregon alone. I had just seen him a month prior. He and Jack were visiting my grandparents in Santa Barbara and I had driven up from LA to see them as well. There was traffic on the way up so I drove directly to the beach where Jack and Dennis were boogie boarding. Dennis was the king of the beach and he looked the part. His entire life he had the same curly shoulder-length and sunkissed hair, a permanent tan and a tank top. His van had been modified by hand. He had taken out the back seat and duck taped folding beach chairs in their place. The car smelled like him, like the ocean.

I sat next to Dennis on the beach and stared out at the ocean.

"Do you know anyone who's transgendering?" He asked while still looking ahead. He wasn't the type of person to talk about the weather, and thank God. Discussing the current wind patterns with anyone is exhausting.

"No, but maybe someone is and I just don't know it." I replied.

"Alright, that's cool. I don't know anyone who is either. It's just wild man." He still spoke like a surfer even in his sixties. He then proceeded to stand up and run full throttle towards the ocean and cannonball into a wave, that would be his bath for the day.

Later that night, a family friend was throwing a party at her house to celebrate the launch of a new Tequila company. I was definitely going as my favorite type of alcohol was free. The party was taking place at the same house I was robbed at six years prior and was the last place on earth Dennis would be seen at. He was too cool to pretend to network with a bunch of CEO's with hair implants who thought Sex Wax was a lubricant. Dennis stayed at my grandparents while the rest of us went on to the party.

I hadn't been back to that house since I was held at gunpoint. It didn't feel the same. This house had always felt like a second home to me, but now, I walked the hallways nervous for who was around the corner.

I don't drink tequila regularly, I can enjoy a margarita but I'd much rather have something that doesn't make me scream "OLAY" everytime I take a sip. But, there was an ice luge filled with tequila and that was something on my bucket list. Not wanting to let myself down, I indulged. Usually when I drink I throw up before I get too drunk, this time I didn't throw up until 3am that morning. I woke up from the guest room bed, leaned over the side and vomited approximately 18 times. I then very calmly placed a towel over my barf and excused myself. I went and slept in the other guest room where someone hadn't soiled the air. Because I am not a cat, I always try to make it to the toilet or at least wood or laminate floors to barf. There was only one other time I didn't make it to the appropriate location.

I got the stomach flu in 2009 in the middle of the night. I climbed down from my bunk bed and walked into my mom's room to wake her up. The bunk bed was a choice I made myself and not something handed down to me. I opened my mom's door and politely awakened her by scream asking if it was ok if I threw up.

"That's ok, you can throw up." She said while walking over to me.

My body took this as a go ahead and I barfed macaroni salad all over her freshly painted walls and got into her bed.

I was now shaming myself for doing this a second time. I laid down in the fresh guest room and felt much better. The best feeling in the world is after you barf and all your nausea goes away and your appetite comes back. Sometimes, this feeling even gives me energy. After laying in bed for a few moments, I decided I should probably go and clean up the massive mess I just made. Instead, I went downstairs and made a turkey sandwich.

The next morning, everything was spinning and then pounding and then wiggling. My grandma had made a beautiful breakfast of eggs benedict and pancakes for everyone to enjoy. The sight of the wobbly poached egg made me regain that same feeling I had before I yakked only a few hours before. Dennis was already packing up the van for the next day at the beach. I wanted nothing more than to not move ever again, so I skipped the beach. I also needed to clean up my vomit upstairs before my grandma found out.

The carpet was white, but not white white, more of a beige white. I used paper towels to dispose of the 'chunks' and then poured bleach directly onto the carpet. The spot was now bright white compared to the rest of the room. Whoopsie. The smell of bleach and barf was going to make me repeat this entire situation so I packed my bags and went back to LA. On my way out of the door I told my grandma I spilled some ice tea on the carpet upstairs and to say goodbye to Dennis for me.

He was the first person after my mom to die and I felt oddly prepared to handle it. I went to work the day after Siri broke the news to me, the memorial wasn't until the following week. I went into Amber's office to ask for a few days off next week to go to the memorial.

"Have you ever been to therapy?" She asked in shock that another member of my family had died.

"No, I don't think I need it." I said as if I hadn't lost about half my family by the age of 22. I was out of a mom and now out of uncles.

"I'm going to pay for you to go, it'll be like health care." She was already texting me her therapists number.

"No, it's fine, I really don't need it."

"Trust me, you need it."

I knew she was right, I did need it. I hadn't even spoken to a family member or friend about anything, I didn't know how I was going to open up to a stranger while sitting on a leather couch.

Therapy to me sounded like something rich divorcees did to occupy their days. I just didn't understand the point. Talking about all the people I had lost wasn't going to bring them back, it was just going to cost me a new pair of boots and the socks that go with them. I didn't want anyone to know I was sad, that I teared up anytime someone even brought up my mom. Therapy was for the weak. I was content bottling up my emotions and using them anytime I needed to cry on command. That was a skill I was planning on using if I ever decided to make a go at Hollywood.

Because Amber was my boss, I listened to her. And she told me I could leave work early every Thursday if I went. I immediately scheduled an appointment for 3pm next Thursday.

I arrived early in Brentwood and waited in my car until it was exactly 4 minutes before my appointment started. I knew the therapist would look for an underlying meaning if I was either late or early, so I had to beat her at her own game and arrive exactly on time.

There was a small waiting room and no receptionist. She had a generous display of InTouch magazines that were actually from this month, so it was off to a good start. The only other door in the waiting room opened and she walked out. There must have been a camera or a glory hole that missed because I still don't understand how she knew I was there, I'm very quiet.

"Gracie? You can come in now." She had large curly hair that hit at the middle of her back. She was wearing a denim jumpsuit and had a floral tattoo poking out at her shoulder. This was not what I was expecting.

I followed her into her office. Again, not what I was expecting. It looked like how I wanted my first apartment to look. Beige walls, string lights, sisal rug. There were no framed Rorschach tests, no chaise lounges and no sense of judgment. It felt comfortable, like somewhere I wouldn't mind spending an hour a week. I took a seat on the large sectional, worried she would sit right next to in an attempt to jump start my trust in her. Instead, she sat across the large coffee table in a reclining chair that was disguised as something from Pottery Barn.

"So, what brings you here?" She asked, no notepad or pen in sight. It felt like we were having a normal conversation, or it did until I opened my mouth.

"My uncle just died and my mom died before and.." I couldn't finish my sentence without bumbling on my words, "and, uhm, other people before that. I'm sorry I'm crying."

"You can cry here." Her permission sent me into a tailspin headed for actual rivers coming out of my eyes. No one had ever given me permission to cry before. I had been told to "stop crying" by many people before and that "crying was not an option at this Chuck-e-Cheese."

She didn't say anything until I composed myself. "Well, I've never been to therapy before." I said warning her for my lack of knowledge on therapy etiquette. I looked around the room again, hoping this time I would find a framed poster telling me what to do next.

She asked me questions that she assumed would be basic, about my family history and the general layout of my life.

"It would be a lot easier if I just emailed you," I said trying to make light of the situation. My family history is rather complicated. If I trace it back far enough for you, we would get into my great-great-grandfather, the murderer. Which actually might be the root of all my problems, but we only had an hour today.

"We don't have to talk about your family if you don't want to, we can talk about anything you want."

"I just want to be able to say my moms name without crying." I said, crying.

"That might never happen, you're never going to move on from your mom's death, and you're not supposed to. Losing a parent isn't something to forget, it isn't something to get over, but I also don't want it to define you. I want you to be able to talk about her and talk about yourself with her, the memories you had and not cry. I'm not here to make you cry, I'm here to help you understand your pain and manage that pain, even turn it into something else."

She lost me, just her saying this was making me cry. I grabbed a tissue and nodded my head as if I understood. How was I going to move on and not move on at the same time? She was beginning to sound like English was her second language.

My mom was all I could think about. Every day I had something to tell her, something to show her, then I would realize that I can't and the cycle of mourning would start all over again.

"What stage of grief do you think I'm in?" I asked.

"I don't think you're in any of the stages, I don't believe in the stages. I don't want you to put your feelings onto a chart. I want you to feel however you feel, but I want you to understand why you're feeling that way."

I forgot that therapists weren't allowed to give you any real answers. I nodded along, already believing I was in the depression phase but sometimes edging on anger.

"I have an assignment for you." She leaned in a little closer to me.

"Like homework?" I asked upset. I thought I was done with that.

"No, you don't have to do it if you don't want to."

"I'll do it." I never backed down from someone handing me an open ended assignment, it was like a test of my willpower and kiss-ass-ness.

"Great. I want you to write a letter. Write a letter to your mom telling her everything you want to tell her now. It can be news that you want her to hear or an update on your life or how you're doing now. Anything you didn't get to tell her, write it."

"OK, I can do that." I lied. I wasn't going to do that, I had better things to do than tear soak a piece of paper, like stand in front of my fridge and eat raw cookie dough.

I left the office feeling the same as I had before, there wasn't any sense of relief that I was looking for. I left with a heavy feeling in my chest that I had wasted my time by pretending. I hadn't told her how heartbroken I was. How every day I worried if she was ok and where she was. How I felt completely alone and abandoned. How unfair I thought the world was, what world would take away a girl's mother when she had no one else to lean on. I decided I would keep my next weeks appointment, do the assignment and open up to her help.

The moment I got home, I pulled out a notebook to write this letter. The notebook was one my mom had given me when I started college. I of course hadn't used it yet.

*Dear mom,*

I began, then crossed it out. I would never write a letter to her that way. Actually, I would never write her a letter to begin with. I wondered if I could text this instead.

*Hi mommy,*

*I'm not ok. I'm sad, I'm so sad all the time. Where are you? Why aren't you here to make all this go away? Why did you get sick?*

I wasn't following the assignment, I was supposed to be telling her things, not asking questions. I crossed out the questions and kept writing.

*I'm sorry I wasn't there for you like I should have been. I wasn't there when you died and I don't know why I wasn't. I shouldn't have listened to you. People told me that you weren't aware of what was happening but I don't believe them, you're always aware. I called you the day before you died and no one would let me talk to you, they told me you were napping. I believed them. I accidentally saw a photo of your dead body on David's phone. I wish I didn't see it because it's all I can see now. This isn't something I should have seen but I did. Why would anyone take a photo of you dead. Grandpa did too, I saw it on his computer once. Usually when I see a photo of a crime scene or a car crash, I can't look away even though I know I shouldn't be starring or googling the words 'Black Dahlia dead body'. But when I saw the photos of you, I never closed my eyes so fast. But it wasn't fast enough.*

*I miss you and I know you miss me. You loved me so much and it makes me sad for you. I'm sad that you loved me so much and then had to lose me. We lost each other. You held on only for me and maybe a little bit for David, but I know it was for me. I feel a little narcissistic thinking of your pain of losing me, of not being able to see me and talk to me and know what I'm doing. No mother loves their child as much as you loved me.*

*I thought about naming my daughter Eleanor, if I have a daughter, you even told me I have to. But I don't think I can handle saying your name every day to someone that isn't you. Maybe her middle name will be Eleanor. But I promise I won't name her something stupid like Sailboat or Ashley.*

*I see butterflies a lot. I wish you chose a different sign because sometimes it feels like I'm seeing butterflies too often and that not every single one can be a sign. But then I remember that it's you and you would be the one to show me a sign every day.*

*I have a lot of stupid stuff to tell you too, like Kylie Jenner being pregnant or the new addition to the Housewives of NYC, but you probably already know all that.*

*I wish you would just come back.*

I didn't sign the letter. I planned on writing more but it hurt, so I didn't. The next week I drove back to my therapy appointment. So far the only thing I liked about therapy was telling people I was going to therapy.

"Did you do the assignment?" The therapist asked.

"No, I didn't have time." I had the letter folded up in my purse but I didn't want even my therapist to know how I really felt. I was defeating the whole point of therapy.

"Ok, well we can do that next week if you want."

We began discussing other issues in my life, like my overwhelming anxiety of being murdered, something I was much more comfortable discussing.

"When did this anxiety begin? Do you remember a moment that your thinking shifted?" She asked.

"I think a lot of it stems from my mom being overprotective when I was a kid. I was always being told to look out for pedophiles and to never trust anyone with a mullet. I would cross the street if I saw someone slightly cross eyed, she made me scared of everyone. And then in high school, I got robbed at gunpoint so that might be something too."

"That most definitely is something. Tell me what happened there."

I told her the story that I had told a hundred times before. It was almost a script at this point.

"I'd like to try something with you to help you to stop picturing this event. Just go with me for this. I'm going to break the story up into parts and number them. The first part is you in the kitchen before anything happened and walking to your room. The second part is seeing the robber for the first time. The third part is him tying you and your friend up. The fourth part is you alone and trying to call for help. The fifth part is him taking you to your mom's room. The sixth part is waiting in the room with him for your friend's parents to get home. The seventh part is hearing them arrive and the robber leaving the room. The eighth part is him bringing her parents into the room and tying them up too. The ninth part is him being taken to the safe. The tenth part is him returning to the room and then walking out the back door."

"Ok, I can do that." I was slightly confused but willing to go along. I would love nothing more than to not picture his eyes in the ski mask every time I went to bed.

She had me practice and memorize what part of the story corresponded to which number. Between the homework assignment and memorization, this was feeling a lot like school.

"Now when I say a number, say the part of the event that corresponds to that number. So if I say four, you say…"

"Alone and calling for help."

"Ok good, are you ready? I'm going to try to move fast, so you can just use a keyword even."

"Ok."

"Two."

"Seeing the robber."

"Eight"

"Her parents coming in the room."

"Ten"

"He leaves."

"Three."

"Ties us up."

She went on through each number three or four times. I somehow managed to keep up. The memory was so ingrained in my brain that this task was easier than if she asked me to tell her what I had for lunch that day.

"Now the story is all mixed up, it doesn't exist anymore, it's just a series of random events in no particular order. Can you still picture the story as clearly as before?"

I pretended to try to strain my brain to remember, "No, it's almost foggy." Of course, I could remember what happened, I was there for it, wasn't I?

"Now when your brain wants to remember what happened to you that night, you have to confuse it. Think of it happening in this impossible order. Now, I'm going to retell the story back to you, but I'm going to mix up the story in each part. For example, I'm going to say that he came into the room and pointed a banana at you. When I say something incorrect, I want you to interrupt me and correct me by saying first 'no silly' then say the correction. So you would say, 'no silly, he came into the room with a gun.'"

She had lost me here, but I still had 25 more minutes before I was allowed to leave. I didn't understand what type of new-age hippie shit this was. I refrained from asking if she learned this from Jim Jones.

I interrupted her during the story as she wished, starting with "no silly," then correcting her, "he tied me up and told me to not move or else he would shoot me in the head." I felt like some sort of little girl explaining how she murdered her parents, giggling every time I had to call my therapist, "silly." I don't even call my dog silly. I became convinced that I was being brainwashed or hypnotized or both. We were just one step away from analyzing my dreams and wearing costumes.

Her experiment ended finally but she failed to explain why I had to call her silly. I guessed that she was again trying to mix up the story in my brain. Maybe I have an above-average brain, but this wasn't going to permanently alter my memory, it was just going to make me look up her credentials. She tried to explain to me the concept of time being circular rather than linear. That if I was able to mix up this timeline, it wouldn't exist in my brain as it had before. I could tell that she was trying to get my guard down, not on my watch. Maybe having me call her "silly" was a way for me to get comfortable with her, to laugh at what had happened. She didn't know that I was constantly laughing at that event, I laughed at everything. Something they don't teach you in therapy is to laugh, so I appreciated her effort.

I left her office that day trying to put the story back into the correct order. I wasn't about to let my guard down, that's how people get murdered. The night of the robbery taught me to be hyper aware of my surroundings and to always lock the doors no matter how fancy the house is. The investigating team discovered the robber had easily entered through an unlocked door in the basement. I learned that the most important thing to do in any life or death situation is to remain calm. Crazy responds well to calm. If any of us had attempted to fight back or not give him what he wanted, I might not be here right now.

I decided that therapy isn't for me. At least not yet, I'm not ready to talk about the hole in my heart, and I might never be. There are some things too painful to be said, some things are better left hidden in the bottom left-hand corner of your heart. There are some things talking about won't fix.

I've noticed that some people turn losing a person into a lesson, as a way to start living a different type of life. The only thing I can say I learned is to cherish your people. Cherish every moment with them. Even when they're telling you "you look fat in red," cherish that moment.

One of the earliest memories I have with my mom, was when I was five years old. It was my first day of kindergarten in Aspen and I didn't know anyone. My mom left me with the teacher after I was shown my desk. I was so excited, it was all mine, it even had my name on it. I sat down in my chair and opened up my backpack. Then, I felt this feeling in my stomach that I still get to this day. It's the feeling of fear and it's deep and unexplainable, but you know what it is. I stood up from my desk, took my backpack and walked out. I sat at the door frame and unpacked my new notebooks and markers there. I wasn't ready to start kindergarten.

The teacher came over and tried to convince me to come back in, but it didn't work. The principal was called and she tried to persuade me as well. Still didn't work. I sat outside the classroom for the entire day, even ate my lunch out there. I continued to do this the entire week. At the end of the week, my mom came to pick me up and was informed of the "situation."

On the car ride home my mom tried to understand why I wouldn't go inside the classroom. I couldn't explain why because I didn't know how to explain the fear I had.

"Go inside when you're ready." My mom told me.

Looking back at that moment can sum up how I feel now. I'm not ready to "go inside" and dig up all the feelings I'm holding onto. I just want to live outside and think about the good times for now. My mom wouldn't want me to be sad, she would want me to go out into the world, eat chocolate croissants and buy a puppy.

Dennis, my mom and me (kinda).

Douriés, my mom and me (kinda).

## Where Ellie Is Now

Here is an email from my mom. She wrote it in 2011 when she was first diagnosed. David sent it to me a few weeks after she passed away. I think this sums up everything quite nicely.

-----Original Message-----
From: David Decret
To: Gracie O'Connell
Sent: Mon, Sep 19, 2016 4:10 am
Subject: FW: Grace regarding where I will be

Hi Graceycakes
Just in case, I do die I want you to know where I am.
I am in heaven watching over you every second of your life. I will see you again grace so don't worry. please just live the life you are supposed to and then when you die, I will see you again.
BUT, in the meantime, I am right here. I know God will take me to heaven bc I think I've been a nice person. I raised the best little girl

229

in the world so I assume that is an entry ticket. Please believe in God, Grace. He is there for you and I will be too.

I know you will be sad but please don't be. please smile when you think of me. I always make you laugh and I want you to continue to laugh and be happy. don't be sad for me. I am okay. I am right here with you. Julie will make you laugh. and jenny. these two people are me. if you miss me, call them bc they are me.

I will be in heaven watching over you and looking in other people's houses. I will start at Versailles and look in all the rooms that are were off limits. then I will go to all the apartments in Paris? the old cool ones and check everything out. this is going to take me years. But, I will always be watching over you.

Also, grace, I will be watching over all the children in the world that need me. Kids who are being abused, neglected, or just being raised badly. I will also watch over any child being bullied. So know that mommy will be happy doing these things while you are happy living a fruitful life.

I will be in all the clouds, in every butterfly, and in every pretty flower. My favorite flower is a peony so every time you see a peony, think of me. Try to keep peonies in your house all the time. You don't have to tell anyone why, it will be our secret. If you get super sad, go to a butterfly conservatory and I will be flying all around you. Also, I will most likely be in a rainbow. I will NOT be in the ocean or any water. It scares me. Also, think of me in Paris, in the Luxembourg Garden where I took you for ice cream. Take your children there and buy them ice cream and tell them it is from me, grandmother. Don't call me grandma. It sounds too hillbilly. Call me grandmother. Grand Mother. I like that.

Here are other places I will be...

the Portuguese church in Rome

In the louvre. most likely in the big red room near the delacroixs. look for me and think of me. be happy.

I will not be in hawaii, it is too far away. just remember the fun we had in hawaii.

in the Palais Royal garden where I took that picture of you with the black and white statues. I ill be here a lot. If you are there, wait, and I will come to you immediately. Look for me in a flower or a bird or a butterfly. I will also be having a cafe creme in a cafe in the palais royal. or I will be by the fountain in the middle.

I will always also be with aunt julie. unless, she is in water. go to julie and you will find me.

I will be with Jenny.

I will also be with david. go to these people if you feel sad.

dont forget me grace. dont bury your sadness and erase me. I am right there with you. please talk to me and tell me everything. everything from a boy you like, to new makeup or shoes you bought. Just keep talking to me. its not weird.

Please look for me grace. Open your heart and your eyes and I am right there. always next to you.

# Acknowledgments

Thank you to my boyfriend, Ty. Thank you for not only proof reading and lending your handwriting for the cover, but for being my favorite person. Thank you for being nice to me even when I'm being mean to you. Thank you for being you.

Thank you to my grandparents, Anne and Dan, for everything. A special thank you to my grandma for always sending me home with chocolate chip cookies and introducing me to CSI.

Thank you to my aunt Heather for making me act like a lady and coming up with the book title.

Thank you to my dad, David for calling me on my bullshit and taking care of me.

Thank you to my dad, John, for always making me feel super duper loved and moving my couch.

Thank you to my dad, Dylan, and Augusta for making me laugh and knocking some sense into me.

Thank you to Heather Robinson (Hbis) for giving me feedback and editing the story.

Thank you to Jenny for Sunday night dinners and teaching me how to order takeout (always ask for extra sauce).

Thank you to Yolanda for jump-starting this book project and being there for me.

Thank you to Eliot for all the adventures we went on and being you.

Thank you to Masie for gossiping with me and being my biggest fan.

Thank you to all the Have Some Decorum readers, this is for you.

Thank you to everyone who works at In N Out, keep it up.

Thank you Paris, for being my home.

Thank you to Debbie and Kelsey Owens, Jack and Cody Dragon, Diandra Douglas, Joey Weber, Louisa Crawford, Ursula and Patrick Nesbitt, Madison Krebs, Sarah and Susan Simmons, Mer James, Christy Nichols, Amber Farr, Randy Jackson, Hollye Jacobs, Sabena and Gage Frink, Kate Burrows, Clementine and Henry Farnum, Chloe Tournier-Decret, Aline Isambert, and everyone who ever dealt with me.

CPSIA information can be obtained
at www.ICGtesting.com
Printed in the USA
BVHW030014230323
660939BV00006B/505

9 781714 119912